Y0-AUZ-604

The Secret World of INTERPOL

"We are in the age of the hunter. This is a James Bond world, a CIA world."
— Marshall McLuhan

The Secret World of
INTERPOL

Omar V. Garrison

WILLIAM MACLELLAN

GLASGOW LONDON NEW YORK LOS ANGELES

Books are published by
William Maclellan,
104 Hill Street,
Glasgow G3 6UA.

First Published in U.K. 1977
Copyright ©Omar V. Garrison
ISBN 08 5335 227 5
Library of Congress Catalogue Card No. 76-24523

Printed in Scotland by Port Seton Offset Printers,
Seton Works, Cockenzie, East Lothian, Scotland.

Contents

> *"The more the Government or any other institution knows about us, the more power it has over us."*
>
> — Sen. Sam Ervin

1. *The Dirty Dossier*

In late 1974, newspapers in the U.S., Britain and West Germany reported that Interpol, "the international crime-fighting organization," was being sued for circulating false information from its secret files.

Named as co-defendants in the suit were the FBI, Scotland Yard, and Germany's Federal Criminal Police Department.

It was the first time in history that the operation of the international police network had been challenged in court. But coming as it did on the heels of Watergate and the disgraceful series of revelations which followed, the story attracted little notice. The public's attention was focused on the horrors still emerging from the ongoing probe into activities of the U.S. intelligence community.

Never in the annals of any nation had so many frightening official acts of government been laid bare to the public scrutiny in so brief a period. The sordid revelations — which, it was to be hoped, would mark an end of political innocence in America — resembled nothing quite so much as the confessions of some sovereign Godfather who had directed a super Mafia.

At one point, in fact, while one agency of the U.S. Government was loudly proclaiming an all-out war against organized crime, another actually established a working liaison with the real Mafia. But there too, efforts of the underworld figures appeared almost harmless when measured against the larger depredations of the Washington-based federal gangsters. The Mafiosi, after all, did not have at their disposal the vast technical and financial resources, nor the above-the-law status of the official agents and spies.

In these circumstances, then, the public was incapable of reacting very strongly to the news that Interpol may have provided an international dimension to the dirty dossier. By that time, a kind of numbness had spread through the body politic.

One aspect of the case, however, did arouse some interest among a handful of observers, including several members of Congress. They asked:

What, exactly, is Interpol's role as an international intelligence network, with access to massive files of information on U.S. citizens.

No one seemed to have a ready answer. In fact, when it came to that, very few even in government appeared to know anything about the history and structure of the Paris-based organization nor of its relation to the many diverse governments which support it.

In the popular mind, Interpol (the cable designation for International Criminal Police Organization) had long been glamorized as a kind of global detective force — Maigrets who roamed the world, tracking down jet-age crooks, counterfeiters and Kingpins of the international drug traffic.

A jacket blurb on the most recent book of this *genre* (published in May, 1976) describes Interpol as "that fabled network of global gendarmes forever at war with the preying powerful of international crime."

In the harsh light of a legal confrontation, however, a wholly different picture emerged. Like the G-men of literary fame (before the FBI Pandora's Box was opened), or Scotland Yard in the never-never world of Sherlock Holmes, Interpol's legendary image is largely composed of myth.

Upon close inspection, Interpol turned out to be a non-governmental league of law-enforcement agents from 122 countries throughout the world, whose membership is sponsored by their respective governments.

It is not an international police force, but rather a communications network engaged in the storage and international disemination of information about individuals, criminal and non-criminal.

The organization itself is responsible to no national government nor sovereign power, but is at the disposal of any of them. In practice, it has been completely flexible in the interpretation of its constitution.

How could it do otherwise when its membership represents many mutually inimical States, some of which are unhampered by the demands of democratic institutions or due process of the law? Ranged alongside each other are democracies (in name, at least) and what U.N. Ambassador Daniel P. Moynihan correctly called "totalitarian Communist regimes and assorted ancient and modern despotisms."

There is Uganda, for example, which is a member, and whose president Big Daddy Amin received a standing ovation in the United Nations following a speech in which he called for the extinction of fellow-member Israel as a State.

The full Interpol roster includes such other strange bedfellows as Algeria, Spain, Roumania, Yugoslavia, Greece, Turkey, Cuba, Bolivia, Vietnam and Taiwan.

Interpol's purpose and the nature of its activities have been variously described by different spokesmen for the organization. In its constitution, adopted in 1946, Interpol describes its function in these words:

"To insure and promote the widest possible mutual assistance between all criminal police authorities within the limits of the laws existing in the different countries and in the spirit of the Universal Declaration of Human Rights."

To this definition an official of the U.S. Treasury Department (the designated representative of Interpol in America), added an important connotation. Replying to a query by Congressman Thomas M. Rees, assistant deputy secretary James B. Clawson explained:

"It [Interpol] provides the mechanism whereby law enforcement authorities can exchange criminal investigation information *and intelligence on matters with international ramifications*, as well as requesting criminal investigation in the member countries." (Emphasis added.)

Later in the same memorandum, Clawson declared more succinctly:

"In essence, Interpol is a clearing house for information, and a communications network."

Interpol has access to files

U.S. involvement with Interpol matters, Clawson said, is based on Treasury's law-enforcement responsibilities and its extensive and close relationships with U.S. law enforcement agencies.

These agencies include the FBI and IRS, both of which figured prominently in the Watergate scandal. Owing to the direct liaison and cross-feed of information among all federal agencies, Interpol also has indirect access to the copious intelligence files of the State Department, the U.S. Customs, Post Office Department, Army and Navy Intelligence, U.S. Coast Guard, Food and Drug Administration and others.

Vigorous denials by the agencies concerned will be answered in the following pages by documented evidence fully supporting the accuracy of our allegation.

In particular, the "mutual assistance" between the FBI and Interpol merits the closest scrutiny.

In the memorandum cited above, the Treasury official acknowledged the accuracy of an earlier report by the Library of Congress Congressional research service, that Interpol's Washington bureau has direct access to the massive, computerized files of the FBI National Crime Information Center (NCIC).

This vast computer complex, which former Massachusetts Governor Francis W. Sargent called "one of the biggest threats to our democratic system," first went into operation in 1966. Since that time, it has grown like all electronic Topsies in our day. It is now linked with a network of 104 control centres deployed through all 50 States and Canada, serving upwards of 4,000 inquiry terminals.

According to a report released by the NCIC Advisory Policy Board on June 11, 1974, "The NCIC system through its related control terminals and the advent of criminal history, has a potential of over 45,000 local, state and federal criminal justice user terminals."

Law enforcement agents not only have available to them upon demand a split-second search of the giant dossier bank in the master computer; but on the State level, they feed their own data into the system.

FBI Director Clarence M. Kelley recently reported that "the

Center's computers have processed as many as 140,000 transactions in a single day."[1]

The one overriding and necessary criterion to justify such a gigantic daily tide of information about U.S. citizens — even within national borders — would be the accuracy of the information that flows into and out of the system.

When and if that prerequisite is met, there still remain the problems of the *kind* of information stored, how long it should be kept, who should have access to it, and what it should be used for.

At the time of this writing there has been very little new legislation or judicial rulings limiting the use of the NCIC — or indeed, of any other law-enforcement computer in America. Such a law is also non-existent in Britain.

As for the primary stricture governing its use — accuracy — the following examples, drawn from many available to the writer, will suffice to make clear the grave dangers inherent in *all* such systems.

Alfred Rozier was the assistant manager of a Detroit supermarket. On his way home from work last year, two police officers in a patrol car ordered him to pull over to the curb, then asked to see his driver's licence. With this in hand, they checked by radiotelephone with FBI's computer at the *National Crime Information Centre*. The read-out indicated that Rozier was a wanted criminal.

Protesting his innocence, Rozier was taken to Detroit's second precinct police station and booked. Thereafter, he spent eleven days in jail before police learned that there had been a mistake in identification. Programmers at the NCIC in Washington had incorrectly combined data from Rozier's file with that of another man of the same name.

Asked why they had not acceded to Rozier's urgent requests that they check his fingerprints, which would prove he was not the wanted man, a department spokesman said:

"The officers probably didn't believe Rozier's protestations of innocence, because they all say they're innocent and besides, the identification numbers matched."

While the guiltless man was being held in jail, he lost his job at the supermarket. His car, which police had left at the spot where he was taken into custody, was stripped and the windows smashed by vandals.[2]

A few months later, it was revealed that similar incidents had occurred across the border in Canada. There it was reported that three Canadians, innocent of any crimes, had on different occasions been jailed because of errors programmed into a central computer installation operated by the Royal Canadian Mounted Police. The data bank is accessible to a number of local forces across the country.

Their names and licence numbers were fed into the Canadian Police Information Centre in Ottowa, which responded with incorrect data identifying them as fugitives from justice.

The motorists were held in jail while the entering agencies that had filed the warrant information were notified that the wanted men had been apprehended.

Although the computer had wrongly branded the men criminals in a matter of seconds, it required several days to determine that the computer print-out was false.

A spokesman for the Ottowa police was quoted as saying later that: "The information in any computer is only as good as the person putting it in or taking it out."[3]

That statement, accurate though it was, may have explained, but it did not excuse, the injustice done to the victims of the blunders.

It would be naive for the reader to assume that because he is a law-abiding citizen, his name is not among the 497,168 computerized "criminal" histories of the NCIC Computer (as of November 1, 1974); or the 55,739,000 index cards to be computerized in the future.

If you have ever had what the FBI terms a "significant" contact with a local or federal law-enforcement agency, you have a record. That record may not be accurate; it could be, like those cited above, mixed with that of some other and less reputable person. It could reflect some long-forgotten, youthful indiscretion. It might be the report of a mistaken arrest or tell only half the story, failing to reveal that you were found innocent of the charges.

According to Sen. Sam Erwin, chairman of the Subcommittee on Constitutional Rights, *an incredible 70% of all arrest records in the U.S. do not include final disposition of the case.* (Emphasis added.)

FBI propaganda vs. facts

In public relations messages, issued by the FBI from time to time to counteract the alarm raised by "privacy paranoids," Americans are assured that the NCIC network is managed and directed "by skilled professionals of the criminal justice system."

The *facts* about the Rozier case and others like it, however, stand out in bold contrast to such assertions.

But what of the additional claim made not long ago by FBI Director Kelley that: "It has indexed *only* the names of individuals for whom arrest warrants are outstanding or persons who have had substantial involvement, supported by fingerprint records, with the criminal justice system."[4] (Italics his.)

Perhaps the most cogent answer to that affirmation is the experience of a resident of Massachusetts. In a letter to the State's governor, the irate citizen wrote:

"A scary thing happened to me last spring. A relative of mine got a job as a deputy sheriff. One bored night on dispatcher's duty, he ran his family through the National Crime Information Center. Ten out of eleven of us were listed."

None of the family had committed a criminal offence. The

deputy's mother was listed because when she was 18, neighbors had complained to police about a noisy party of young people at her house. His stepfather's name was in the computer because he had once reported receiving a bad check. And so on.[5]

Deeply disturbed by the threat to individual liberty posed by the NCIC's automated injustice, Massachusetts formally withdrew from the FBI computer link-up. Top officials of both Pennsylvania and Iowa are also presently reviewing their States' participation in the network.

While Massachusetts like many other States today, operates its own criminal history computer, it has passed legislation setting up a civilian board to supervise the files stored in it. The new statute bans the entering of an arrest record unless that arrest resulted in a conviction.

Moreover, access to the files is strictly limited, and each individual who is represented in the data bank has the statutory right to inspect his own dossier. If he discovers inaccuracies, the law requires that such false information be deleted or corrected.

No one in an open society such as ours, or very few, would question such a right, if justice is to have any meaning. Yet when directors of a federally financed data-bank program recommended that a citizen should be permitted to see and, if necessary, to correct his own file, the FBI firmly vetoed the idea.

The tenacity with which the FBI will cling to an arrest record, even when the subject is innocent, is clearly shown in the case of Dale Menard, a former Marine. The FBI fought for five years through four courts to keep from removing from their files an arrest record based on the fact that Menard had been taken into custody on suspicion of burglary. It had been established almost immediately that he was guilty of nothing more than being in the neighborhood where residents had reported a prowler.

Rapid growth in data exchange

In addition to the extensive criminal history files, the FBI maintains an undisclosed number of other records, which are fully exchanged with law-enforcement agencies of foreign countries through Interpol's U.S. Central Bureau.

During the fiscal year 1973, for example, Interpol's National Central Bureau in Washington was "in communication" with the NCBs of 89 foreign countries. A total of 3918 foreign and domestic investigative requirements were processed reflecting a 69% increase over the previous year.

According to the same official report, "in addition to the investigative requests handled by the NCB [in Washington] 1,956 intelligence items received from foreign NCBs were forwarded to the United States enforcement agencies having jurisdiction or interest. The total workload of the NBC, 11,605 outgoing pieces of correspondence consisting of both investigative requests *and intelligence items*, reflects a 40% increase over Fiscal Year 1972."[6] (Italics added.)

The dramatic increase in information flow reflected in the above statistics should be a cause for considerable concern. It is significant that during the given year in which these thousands of communications passed back and forth between the Washington NBC and the police of 89 countries, only 82 arrests were made as a consequence of the exchange.

It is logical to assume that a considerable portion of the "intelligence items" represent personal documentation resulting from covert data gathering by various government agencies.

Some of these sensitive records concerning U.S. citizens were supplied to countries which do not have diplomatic ties with the United States.

In the case of Soviet-bloc countries, this information could be made available to the Russian secret police (KGB), to cite but one example. In all instances, once released to foreign law-enforcement agencies (some of which are the political arms of their regimes), the confidential material is beyond the control of the originating bureau. It is beyond the jurisdiction of U.S. courts, Congressional committees, or any other regulatory body.

In short, the unrestricted practice of personal record-keeping has assumed global proportions. Such dossiers provide a potential tool for blackmail by espionage agents abroad and the means of suppressing dissent at home.

Defending the discretion of the NCB personnel, Kenneth S. Giannoules, former chief of Interpol's U.S. bureau, loftily told Timothy McGovern of radio station KPFK in Los Angeles: "The United States Interpol bureau is staffed by U.S. federal enforcement officers, and not international employees."

Few persons who recall the dismal record of federal agents as revealed recently before Congressional committees and in the media, would find much reassurance in Chief Giannoules's statement. To many, it is like saying that our jewels are guarded by a team of well-known burglars.

Consider, by way of example, a legal suit currently pending before the U.S. District Court in Washington. It was brought by an Afghan diplomat named Muhammad Sami, against the U.S. Government; Interpol ("an alien association doing business at the Department of the Treasury"); Louis B. Sims, chief of Interpol's U.S. bureau; and his deputy, James O. Holmes.

Sami charges that the "skilled professionals" who direct Interpol's U.S. operation, transmitted from IP-Washington to various European and Middle Eastern countries numerous cables containing false and defamatory information about him.

Specifically, what had happened was that Interpol Washington had rashly and improperly stepped into a child custody fight between Sami and his American wife. Acting on the Interpol circulations stating that the U.S. wanted Sami arrested for an extraditable offense, the police of West Germany arrested Sami and held him in jail for four days. He was released only after the U.S. State Department intervened.

One significant fact which emerged from the case was contained in a letter written May 22, 1975 by K.E. Malborg, assistant legal adviser of the U.S. State Department.

Addressed to Louis B. Sims, Interpol's bureau chief in Washington, the letter noted that the Sami case was not the first instance of people being falsely arrested on Interpol orders.

"From time to time in the past," wrote Malmborg, "we have had difficulty with people being arrested abroad for extradition on instructions from Interpol."

The letter noted that in the Sami case, the offense of which he was accused (violation of a Maryland court order regarding custody of his children) is not even extraditable.

The State Department official pointedly observed that before requesting foreign police to make provisional arrests, State assures itself that: (a) there is an extradition treaty with the other country; (b) that the offense is covered by the treaty; and (c) that the local authorities asking the arrest have the agreement of the Governor or the Attorney General to follow through with the extradition.

Had Interpol's Washington bureau followed this procedure, Muhammed Sami would not have been falsely arrested in Germany.

Secret files exposed in 40s

The insidious evils of government spying and the maintenance of secret dossiers have been in clear evidence on the national scene for over two decades — ever since the loyalty trials of the 40s. That was when, over the protests of J. Edgar Hoover, the public first had a brief glimpse into some of the FBI's confidential files.

Before the row-upon-row of steel file cabinets were made secure once more against outside inspection, it was revealed that along with data on spies, Communists and criminals, the FBI "investigative reports" also contained unevaluated information concerning millions of citizens innocent of any kind of lawbreaking.

The material, accumulated by the Bureau's faceless legion over an undisclosed period of time included cocktail gossip, unverified rumors and reports by self-appointed neighborhood gestapos. The files bulged with detailed accounts of each individual's intimate affairs: what he had said to a close friend in an unguarded moment, what he had written in private correspondence, the state of his business interests, his sexual habits. An unidentified man in Arlington, Virginia had notified the FBI that one of his neighbors often entertained army officers at lively parties, and speculated that he might be obtaining military information and passing it on to a foreign power. About once a month "an unknown individual in civilian clothes, appearing to be a foreigner, attended the gatherings." Moreever, his 11 year-old son had reported seeing the same neighbor appear on his porch virtually nude to pick up his newspaper. This weighty bit of intelligence was duly inserted into the FBI dossier.

These initial disclosures were brought about by the trial of Judith Coplon, a secretary accused of trying to pass abstracts of classified documents to the Russians. FBI Chief Hoover was vehemently opposed to the files being introduced into the court proceedings, but the alternative was to allow Miss Coplon to go free. Hoover's objection was overruled by the then-Attorney General Tom Clark.

Answering critics who were deeply concerned that the vast accumulation of intrusive personal information revealed by the Coplon trial might one day be used to pressure individuals or groups for political ends, Mr. Hoover promised special security measures. He insisted that keeping the files safe from improper use was, in effect, a sacred trust.

It has now been learned that in 1964, the same J. Edgar Hoover arranged to have an unsavoury report on the love life of the late civil rights leader Martin Luther King, disseminated to the media. The file consisted of material picked up and put on tape by an FBI electronic bug planted in hotel bedrooms used by Dr. King.

In addition to sending copies of the tape to newspapers (where all editors rejected them), the FBI chief had a copy also sent to Mrs. King in such a manner that it could not be traced back to the FBI.

A former, high-ranking official of the Bureau said that Hoover believed that sending the tape to Mrs. King would silence her husband's criticism of the FBI and at the same time break up his marriage. It did neither.

The preceeding "dirty trick" by the FBI is not an isolated instance of the kind. A U.S. Senate subcommittee investigating federal intelligence programmes has turned up evidence of a wide variety of illegal activities by the Bureau. Sen. Frank Church, the committee chairman, has expressed a particular interest in the private files assembled by Hoover on scores of prominent public officials. Some of the more sensitive of these files disappeared after Mr. Hoover's death in 1972. At this writing, their whereabouts and contents are still a mystery.

A careful review of FBI's past and continuing mass surveillance and documentation of people is important within the context of the present work because of the Bureau's close liaison with Interpol and with other agencies of the federal government who are also engaged in wholesale espionage.

"So tangled is Washington's subterranean world of spying, intelligence gathering and undercover investigation," reported *Time* magazine, "that any abuse found in one agency seems destined to expose related illegalities in others."[7]

Reflected in some of the Interpol files to be examined in the course of the following chapters are non-criminal data (much of it false) from the secret dossiers of the IRS, CIA, U.S. State Department, Coast Guard, Food and Drug Administration, Naval Intelligence, U.S. Air Force, Post Office Department, FBI and others.

Recent documentary evidence supports charges by libertarians that the same situation exists in Britain. There Scotland Yard maintains a close liaison with Interpol to which agency it transmits information derived from such internal sources as the Home Office, the C-11 (a police intelligence unit), the Swansea driver-licensing computer, Civil Service files, and local government records, as well as that received from the U.S. and elsewhere.

The whole question of Interpol — its history, personnel and role as an international clearing house for intelligence — was first brought into public view in 1973 by the controversial Church of Scientology, one of the organizations that has appeared on the now-notorious Nixon administration hate list.

The reason for the church's presence on the list is still obscure, since unlike the other religious bodies that shared that distinction, the Scientologists have never engaged in any political activity whatever. The sect's membership embraces the full ideological spectrum; and party affiliation is irrelevant to the practice of the church's precepts.

At the same time, both the administrative staff, and the church's founder, L. Ron Hubbard, have waged a vigorous fight against their powerful enemies in various countries throughout the world. In the course of that prolonged and costly strife, they have developed a quite remarkable case study. It covers almost every aspect of the civil liberties issue, from petty harrassment by individuals to full-scale persecution by Parliaments and governmental agencies.

A single example will serve to indicate the staggering magnitude of the legal and extra-legal actions taken against this unorthodox denomination.

For over 20 years, the U.S. Internal Revenue Service has conducted an intensive and continuing investigation of the Church of Scientology and its founder. During that time its agents have amassed a 30,000-page file (it requires 1,500 pages just to list the documents!) yet, after all this time and enormous expenditure of taxpayer money — more than could ever be realized in any taxes recovered from the church — the government has not convicted anyone of anything.

Recently, at an IRS conference, at which Chief Counsel Meade Whitaker met with top legal and investigative aides, after jointly assessing the status of the government's case against the church, Whitaker reportedly declared:

"It is obvious that whatever we are going to do, we are not ready to do it."

Most fair-minded readers would agree, I think, that if IRS hasn't been able to "do it" in twenty long years, perhaps they should not do it at all.

It is beyond the scope of the present work to present a detailed account of the Church of Scientology and of its defense against well-organized attempts to discredit it throughout the world. I have already published a documented study of the subject in another book.[8]

What concerns us here is not the merits or shortcomings of Scientology, but the implications of their experience with a little-known, international intelligence agency called Interpol, and its multi-national connections.

History and creed of Scientology

To provide a proper perspective for the Interpol story which follows, I will attempt a brief summary of the church's history and creed at this point.

Scientology is a new religion evolved from a formulation called *dianetics*, "the modern science of mental health," originated by L. Ron Hubbard in the early 50s.

"The essence of Scientology," wrote Hubbard, "is its practicality: its application is broad and its results are uniformly predictable."

Like initiates of the ancient mystery schools, Scientologists are guided through a course of disciplined study and practice marked by clearly defined stages or degrees.

Hubbard described his earlier work, Dianetics, as an evolutionary step, a tool useful for arriving at a higher level of knowledge. The higher methodology was Scientology which, while retaining the main functions of dianetics, introduces a new soul concept — that of the Thetan (a designation derived from the Greek letter *theta* to distinguish the Scientology precept from traditional interpretations of that word.)

The Thetan is the person himself and is separable from the body. It works through the body and the mind to effect changes in the physical universe, which is called MEST, an acronym formed by the first letters of matter, energy, space, and time.

Some of the statements the Scientologists themselves have used to define and clarify their creed are:

"Man is by nature basically good. He indulges in aberrative or evil behaviour because of traumatic past experiences stored in the memory bank of his reactive mind, once known as the subconscious."

"All the Church's activities are directed toward freeing the Spirit of man."

"Scientology believes the world as a whole requires religious freedom to survive. It's goal is a civilization without insanity, without criminals and without war."

The church is a legally constituted body and has been judicially declared a bona fide religion by a U.S. District Court.

The Scientology movement embraces a broad programme of social reforms, including a campaign against maltreatment of mental patients; a programme for rehabilitating drug addicts; a commission dedicated to correcting abuses by law enforcement agencies; a crusade for improved methods in education, and so on.

Despite all these good works, and in part because of them, Scientology has aroused intense opposition by individuals, organized groups and certain powerful vested interests.

"It is little wonder," wrote columnist William Willoughby of the Washington, D.C. *Star-News,* "with a church that is tackling abuses in medicine, mental health; IRS pressure tactics, interception of mail, phone tapping, the planting of false press releases by government agencies and the dissemination of — and refusal to correct — disinformation and misinformation by the FBI and other police agencies, that the Scientologists are on the enemy lists.

"They've probably got gold stars beside their name."

Another factor which provides an abrasive element in Scientology is the youthfulness of its adherents. The majority are under 35. Parents and relatives have objected strenuously — usually to some governmental or police agency — that their loved ones have fallen into the clutches of "a kooky cult."

Given the volatile and activist nature of the age group attracted to Scientology, it is not surprising that a number of the youngsters who wander into and out of the church's centers are "bad apples." Some are on drugs, some have criminal records, some are sexually disturbed. Even if these individuals have no more than a slight brush with Scientology through an acquaintance who is a member, that fact is duly entered in their file when they are arrested. The church is blamed for the young offender's deliquency.

Over the past quarter of a century, a "dirty dossier" of truly gargantuan size has been built up and circulated among government agencies of a dozen countries where the fast-spreading new religion has taken root.

The Scientologists first learned that Interpol had leaked false information from that agency's secret files when a derogatory article about the church appeared in the German magazine, *Neue Revue* in 1973.

The church traced the "black propaganda" contained in the German publication back through Interpol channels, from the German Criminal Police in Wiesbaden to Scotland Yard in London and eventually to its initial point of dissemination, the FBI in Washington.

We shall have occasion later to examine the original sources of this report's contents, as well as its widespread, international circulation. Eventually, the derogatory and largely false intelligence was passed on by the media to millions in various European countries.

It is important to bear in mind that neither the founder of the Church of Scientology nor any member of its ministerial staff had ever been convicted of a crime. For that reason, the leak was embarrassing to Interpol, which maintains officially that the agency is concerned in the transmission only of criminal histories.

It was hardly unexpected, in these circumstances, that almost everyone along the Interpol lines denied responsibility for releasing the secret dossier. But, as one member of the German legal profession tartly observed:

"It was certainly not an 'act of God' which had the contents of the report distributed to millions of Germans, Austrians, Swiss, Danes, Swedes, and so on."

Investigation, in fact, revealed that the prime mover in the affair was the Max Planck Institute, which had been publicly criticized by the church. Like the mental health associations in other countries that were at war with Scientologists, the Max Planck Institute wielded considerable influence in official quarters.

Through the mediation of the German Ministry of Youth, Family and Health, a request was made to the Ministry of the Interior, which oversees the Federal Criminal Office, for a report on the Church of Scientology.

Drawing upon the Interpol files, Dr. Horst Herold, chief of the Criminal police, provided two copies of the defamatory report to the Minister of the Interior. The latter passed them on to the Family Ministry, which in turn, made them available to the Max Planck Institute.

The police chief later admitted to a Weisbaden court that he had compiled the report "in order to protect the reputation of German psychiatry." This was tantamount to acknowledging that the dossier had been released deliberately to be used as a weapon against the church by the Max Planck Institute.

A legal brief, filed by the church's German lawyers, notes:

"It is a striking fact that the Family Ministry passed the report on to the Max Planck Institute without any mark as to its confidential character. By such an omission the Max Planck Institute was practically given the green light to dispose of the information according to its own discretion."

After using the report in a legal proceeding, one of the Institute's representatives made it available to Constanze Elsner, a newspaper reporter.

To keep the ball rolling, after she had worked the story over, according to court testimony, Miss Elsner then handed the report to Jakob Andersen, another journalist who wrote for a Danish publication, *Ekstra Bladet*, described as "a boulevard paper with strong pornographic tendency."

Additional copies went to journalists in Cologne and Amsterdam, and to an evangelical clergyman named Haack, who was writing a book in which he attacked the Church of Scientology.

Even a Dutch janitor, a Mr. Nebbeling, acquired a copy. Nebbeling, an employee of the Social-psychological Institute of Utrecht, supplied the material to journalists in Belgium, who published exerpts from it in the magazine *Humo* (issues of July 11 and 18, 1974) and the *Journal d'Europe* (April 4, 1974).

Among the false allegations contained in the Weisbaden report, and derived from an FBI dossier on August 13, 1968, were the assertions that:

   a) The church oppresses people by murder threats.

   b) L. Ron Hubbard, the sect's founder is hopelessly insane.

   c) Scientology blackmails its parishioners, using information gained during intimate pastoral counseling.

   d) The church uses drugs in its ceremonies.

Not one of these assertions is based upon criminal or court records. They consist, in fact, of covertly compiled rumor, malicious gossip, and disinformation deliberately launched by the sect's enemies.

The original FBI document opened with the amazing admission that "This agency has not conducted any investigation into Hubbard . . .". Yet the Bureau did not hesitate to put into international circulation the derogatory statements which followed. By releasing the report through official police channels, i.e., through Interpol, the FBI in effect placed the imprimatur of the U.S. Government upon it.

Agencies act without authority

It is legitimate to ask: by what authority does any federal agency — whether FBI, CIA, State Department, IRS or others — make available to foreign instrumentalities non-criminal information concerning U.S. citizens, whether as individuals or groups?

The answer is that it is done without authority and almost always without the knowledge of the person or organization involved.

When in early 1975, this disquieting situation came to the attention of Senator Joseph M. Montoya, chairman of the subcommittee on Treasury, Postal Service and General Government, he asked Secretary of the Treasury Simon to provide him with a detailed explanation of Interpol and the function of the Treasury Department as the U.S. representative.

Noting that the National Commission of Law Enforcement and Social Justice had submitted a documented history of Interpol to him, Sen. Montoya wrote:

"The study raises many serious allegations concerning the organization, its role as an international intelligence network, and its access to data on millions of United States citizens contained in the National Crime Information Center computer."

Sen. Montoya did not receive a prompt response to his query, as requested — at least, not directly. About a week later, he did receive a letter from David R. Macdonald, assistant secretary in charge of enforcement operations. It did not refer to Sen. Montoya's letter of February 6, 1975, however, but to a story which had appeared in the Washington *Star-News* concerning the questions raised about Interpol. The story had quoted a member of Sen. Montoya's staff as saying that the lawmaker had indicated his concern over the question.

The Treasury official chided the Senator for giving the matter a serious thought.

"I was deeply disappointed to read the *Star-News* article last weekend in which you identified yourself with totally baseless charges against Louis Sims (U.S. representative of Interpol) and Treasury Department personnel," Macdonald wrote.

Then, after stating — incorrectly — that Interpol "is a criminal information exchange agency now under the sponsorship of the United Nations," and inviting the Senator to visit the Treasury Department to observe Interpol in operation, he continued:

"It is most unfortunate, however, that you were misled into lending credence to the allegations of the so-called 'Church of Scientology' by your comment to the press without investigating the origin of that organization, its membership, source of funds and real activities."

Clearly irked by the arrogant attitude reflected in Macdonald's letter, Sen. Montoya once more wrote directly to Treasury Secretary William E. Simon:

"I recently received a letter from David R. Macdonald, Assistant Secretary for Enforcement, Operations, and Tariff Affairs. I assume this letter was written without your knowledge, so I am enclosing a copy for your information. I am also enclosing a copy of the press releases which went out from my office.

"The tone of the letter from Assistant Secretary Macdonald concerns me greatly. I listened to the questions of the group who came to me with the same courtesy which I would show to any citizen. These people are apparently sincerely concerned for the protection of their own and other persons' rights and privacy. That is certainly a legitimate concern, and they are well within their rights under the First Amendment in appealing to me for help in understanding the procedures and operations of Interpol."

As for Mackdonald's suggestion that the Senate subcommittee investigate the church rather than Interpol, Sen. Montoya concisely brought the issue back into focus.

"The origin of the church, its membership, its source of funds, or its activities have nothing to do with whether or not the Interpol organization is given information contained in the National Crime Information Center computer or whether foreign member nations of Interpol are provided private information concerning American citizens."

On March 10, 1975 — more than a month after Sen. Montoya's request for information — Secretary Simon responded with a memorandum, "Facts Concerning Interpol."

Some of the data offered by Treasury as "facts," however, did not square with documented information supplied by critics of Interpol. The more important of these disputed points — the history and function of Interpol, its access to FBI records, its Nazi association; its Watergate connection, and

Communist countries' open sesame to Interpol files — will be covered in later chapters.

We must first, however, look more closely at the technical means available for file-building on a grand and global scale. Specifically, we will examine that great machine, par excellence, of modern despotism — the computer.

"Man is born free, but everywhere he is on tape."

—Malcolm Warner and Michael Stone

2. *"The Quiet Peril"*

Computer technology poses the single greatest threat to human liberty in the world today.

It is a problem which, as U.S. Congressman Barry Goldwater, jr. observed, is more far-reaching than any aspect of Watergate. He correctly called it "the quiet peril," because its advance during recent years has been insidious.

Involved in the question of computerized files and related mass surveillance are practices which go to the heart of civil liberty as we understand it in the free world. Yet, the exact nature of what is happening has not been fully recognized.

During the past two decades, the totalitarian potential inherent in permanent secret files on private citizens has been dealt with at some length by civil libertarians, sociologists and legislative committees. From the first, however, the whole issue has been treated as "invasion of privacy."

Probably the label got permanently applied to the issue because of the famous statement by U.S. Justice Louis D. Brandeis, "the right most valued by civilized men is the right to privacy."

However, the issue no longer involves merely a question of privacy as it is generally understood. It is far more serious than that.

The growing documentation of the individual has become a worldwide system of mass surveillance.

Such a system provides a ready and efficient means of social manipulation and control. It is the indispensable tool for silencing dissent and for enforcing blind obedience to the dictates of government.

It would be a simple matter indeed, by use of integrated data banks, to transform today's bureaucratic shepherding of society into tomorrow's dictatorial coercion. Centralized government is already moving swiftly in that direction.

Power to dominate and control

Two British writers, who viewed this problem with 20-20 vision, have reminded us that all information is itself power:

"When its inherent power is coupled to computer power, and men have the ability to handle and disseminate information in quantities and at speeds hitherto inconceivable, one may be certain that the lives of private citizens will be affected. The prospect also exists of this double-power being used to dominate and to control. The capability exists and therefore a dicision is needed to refrain from using it."[1]

The staggering dimensions of this capability are still not

widely recognized. Owing to the swift advance in computer technology, it is now entirely feasible to create data banks with high-speed interfaces, which can monitor the life details of entire populations. A government watch on 200 million Americans is already a technical possibility.

Moreover, the trend is in that direction. The authoritative work on computers cited above, further notes that:

"The capability for computer power 'on tap,' and for information in bulk, will become more widespread very rapidly. When retrieving devices, which need be little more complex than an electric typewriter, are linked to a fact-filing computer, the data from its memory can be sent to remote devices over telephone lines, radio waves, or even laser beams, at speeds measured in minute fractions of a second. One central source — or more likely, several intercommunication computer sources — can hold all the information an organization needs, or a nation needs, *and make it available to anyone, anywhere, anytime, immediately."* (Italics added.)

To take comfort, then, in the thought that an organization like Interpol will not have the financial means for several years at least, to build a huge computer installation at its Paris headquarters, would seem naive. For a modest investment in a machine "little more complex than an electric typewriter," the global police network can have at its command whatever data their colleagues see fit to release to them from the vast information reservoirs in the U.S., Britain, Germany, Japan and elsewhere.

Just how enormous that combined memory bank is in the U.S. alone may be judged from a recent report by Theodore J. Jacobs, director of Ralph Nader's Center for Study of Responsive Law. He noted that, with an estimated *six billion files,* the federal government is the largest single creator and collector of information in the world.

The U.S. General Accounting office estimated that it costs 15 billion a year to maintain these records. The files, said the

GAO, if laid end to end, would stretch the 5,600 miles from Washington to Cairo, and wryly suggested that the ocean depths between these two points might be a good place to bury about 40% of them.

Even in the restricted area of personal dossiers, as distinct from other kinds of data, a survey conducted by the Senate Subcommittee on Constitutional Rights in 1974 brought to light the sobering fact that 54 federal agencies in the U.S. maintain 858 computerized data banks in which are stored a total of 1,245,699,494 files.

It was found that most of these agencies had no explicit authority to collect and store such information.

While many of the departments could legitimately claim that by installing an electronic data processing system, they would save time and money and operate more efficiently, others appear to have been motivated by different considerations. The *New York Times* reported that several Government spokesmen told an interviewer that they believed their own agencies' acquisition of computers was "for playing games."[2]

Once established, the expensive equipment must justify the investment by cost-efficient operation. In other words, a kind of Parkinson's law goes into effect. The greater a given computer's capacity, the more information about individuals must be programmed, stored and retrieved.

One method of keeping the machines and their technicians busy is a lively exchange of information among the hundreds of multi-access data banks. If the one and a quarter billion files previously mentioned seemed overwhelming, let the reader bear in mind that that figure was limited to federal systems. It does not take into account the millions of other dossiers now maintained by State and local governments, to say nothing of the private sector.

In the U.S. even on a regional level, agencies possess personal record systems of impressive size. For example, Santa Clara county in California has installed computer-operated files which can respond to enquiries in a matter of seconds on any one of more than 200,000 residents in that area.

Large cities like Los Angeles, New York and Chicago have similar electronic archives.

The State of New York has set up a coordinating data bank to serve as a master "information handler" for various agencies of the state government. Known as the New York Identification and Intelligence System (NYSIIS), it stores millions of files which are instantly available to 3,600 criminal justice agencies plugged into the computer.

California also has a busy, statewide coordinating data-bank system.

With the help of federal funding through the Law Enforcement Assistance Administration, other states, counties and municipalities throughout the U.S. are installing computerized filing systems.

Although the public has been given the usual platitudes about safeguards, the fact is that few of these data centres have effective controls against unauthorized access. The information stored in them is available through the "buddy" system to a huge number of peace officers, district attorneys, regulatory agencies, welfare bureaus, private investigators, and even to credit reporting companies.

When these functionally separate computers are eventually linked together (and it can be confidently predicted that they will be), they will comprise a vast electronic dragnet covering the nation — ultimately, the entire globe.

Government cover-up

Government officials have put forward a variety of reasons, technical and otherwise, why this great synchro-mesh will never happen.

Anyone who believes that is a good prospect for membership in the Flat Earth Society.

Experience has shown that the degree of trust which can safely be placed in such official reassurances is virtually nil. Alan F. Westin, noted authority on civil liberties, reports that when he interviewed a high Treasury official in February 1964, "I was told that Treasury 'does no wiretapping, period.' As for the new miniaturized listening and transmitting devices, the Treasury official said that these were 'too costly' for the Treasury's limited budget — 'we can't even afford enough two-way radios for our men to contact each other. The manufacturers come and show us their gadgetry, but we can't afford to buy it.' "[3]

My own researches revealed that at the very time this interview took place, official Treasury records showed that from December 1960 to May 1964, the Washington sales office of a single manufacturer of electronic devices sold the Internal Revenue Service a total of $43,876.42 worth of spy gear. It is still not known how many other purchases of similar equipment IRS had made then — and since then — from more than two score makers of intrusion apparatus.

Prof. Westin goes on to point out that following his discussion with the top Treasury official, it was disclosed that throughout the 1950s and 1960s, Treasury maintained a school at its building in Washington, in which IRS agents were taught to tap telephone wires, build and plant radio-transmitter devices and pick locks for surreptitious entry. In addition, IRS agents attended a course on "technical" investigation given by Army Intelligence at Ft. Holabird, Maryland.

Lance J. Hoffman, a leading authority on computers said not long ago that the apprehension among some segments of the public about huge memory banks which contain personal dossiers is well-founded from the technological point of view.

"At least two firms have already delivered as standard product bulk memories which can store in a small area a one-page dossier on each of the 200 million citizens of the U.S.

and retrieve a piece of information at random in under ten seconds."[4]

That was the situation in 1973, presumably with machines that use the conventional ferrite-core memories. Since that time, Bell Telephone Laboratories have announced that after several years research, they have developed the first "working, fully populated magnetic-bubble memory." On two tiny substrates which together can fit into the palm of a man's hand, it can store about 500 million bits of information.

The magnetic-bubble memory can move data at the rate of 700,000 bits per second and provide a full read-write cycle in 5.1 microseconds. Access is accomplished in 2.7 milliseconds.

According to some computer scientists, the new magnetic bubble can shrink the size of a total system as presently designed from half a floor to the size of a suitcase.

"The goal has been to develop thin crystalline planes of magnetic material that could hold about 1,000,000 domains per square inch, or the equivalent of about 100 pages of text. Potentially, stacks of such memories holding as much as 100,000,000 bits per square inch, could store massive amounts of information that would be instantly accessible to computers, at a fraction of the cost of such devices as disks and drum storage units."[5]

As the cost of these memories is thus reduced by advances in computer technology, it will become economically feasible to store ever greater amounts of textual, personal information.

The magnetic bubble described above is not an isolated breakthrough in the swift development of computer science. The U. S. Navy, for instance, is developing a new computer component called a "crosstie memory," which may eventually allow 70 million bits of information to be stored in a square inch of thin, magnetic film.

Another international computer firm has already built a laser memory system that offers a 1,000,000,000,000,000-bit stor-

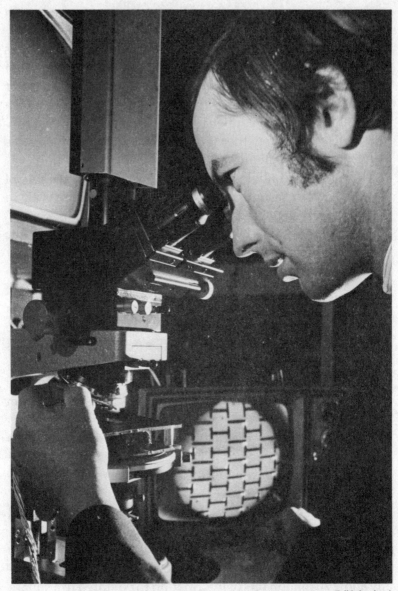

(Bell Labs photo)

Research scientist Robert H. Morrow checks revolutionary new magnetic-bubble memory that will be used in future computers. The memory can move data at the rate of 700,000 bits per second and provide a full read-write cycle in 5.1 microseconds.

age in 60 square feet of floor space. According to the manufacturer, the system provides permanent, nondegrading (in a technical sense) records, easy updating and selective retrieval of data based on any number up to 15 of different criteria. Such has been the amazing acceleration of computer technology that not only the general public, but even the greater part of people who work in that field, have been left behind.

At what was termed "the most decisive" conference of the British Computer Society in the first part of October 1975, the question was put to the members: "Should Information Systems Be Allowed?"

That, observed an IBM lecturer on computer technology afterwards, was indeed "shutting the stable door after the horse has bolted — sired a new generation and died of old age."

A radical transformation

The residual import of all this is simple and can be stated simply:

The present epoch is one of those critical periods in history during which a radical transformation occurs in the social structure of a civilization.

At the root of that transformation in our day is the computer, — with its mass storage of dossiers, providing the means for total surveillance.

To understand fully what this means in terms of the relationship between government and the governed, it is necessary to examine the legal foundation of our liberties.

We are witnessing the gradual supplanting of the Anglo-Saxon concept of government, — running back more than 750 years to the Magna Carta, — with an inquisitorial spy-system distinctive of all totalitarian regimes.

Our Western, democratic theory of justice is based on what

is known as accusatorial law. This is a form of social control in which legislative enactments or legal statutes merely define what constitutes an unlawful *act* and prescribe a penalty if the offender is found guilty by a court of competent jurisdiction. The alleged criminal is publicly accused of an offense and is tried in public by a judge who is not the prosecutor as well. The prosecutor represents the people (or the Crown) and the state does not take sides, but renders judgment based on the evidence. The defendant can confront and cross-examine his accusers. He is considered innocent until proven guilty.

By contrast, under a system of inquisitorial procedure, a body of official spies — secret agents and police — establish a pervasive surveillance over the citizenry with the object of not only discovering criminal acts, but of compelling obedience to governmental will, as determined by the authorities in power. Individual rights and constitutional guarantees are are consistently flouted in seeking information or enforcing conformity.

The inquisitorial government is an avid collector of data from personal lives, much of it derogatory and derived from spiteful informers, gossip-mongers, calumny, suspicion and conjecture.

The tainted material of these dossiers can then be used in various ways against the individual, who does not know what is in such a file and cannot effectively defend himself against it. The whole procedure violates the cardinal principle of common law, that a person must be faced openly with his accusers and that accusations must be known to him.

The masters of Nazi Germany were fervent file-keepers. Wilhelm Hoetl, head of the Security Office in Berlin, tells us that Reinhard Heydrich, the notorious "Hangman of Poland," and wartime president of Interpol, made a particular point of delving into the antecedents of all leading personalities of the Third Reich "in the hope of digging out some weakness he could turn to his own advantage." When no past wrongdoing or serious defect in character could be found, a false report would be introduced into the dossier, to be used when needed, at some future date.

It has been likewise observed that Adolf Eichman was also a meticulous record-keeper who sent countless thousands to the gas chamber by way of his filing cabinets.

"It is frightening indeed to imagine," wrote the authors of *The Data Bank Society*, "What the Nazis *could* have accomplished if they had had electronic storage systems categorizing the whole population, recording its movements and its affiliations and its sympathies; few opponents or 'non-persons' would have survived."

The Communist authorities of Soviet Russia have carried on where the Nazis left off. Secret archives of the KGB (Russian secret police) are filled with intelligence files stuffed with investigative reports, not only on Soviet citizens, but foreigners as well.

In *KGB*, a documented account of the Soviet secret service, John Barron relates a typical instance of the way the police-state dossier is used.

Agents of the KGB had compiled an extensive personal file on a young American studying as an exchange student in Moscow. Their meticulous investigations had revealed that he was a brilliant scholar who in the future would probably fill an important post in the U.S. government or at a leading university. His services as a spy for Russia would be invaluable.

In a locked interrogation room, an official of the secret police accused him of being a CIA plant, but agreed to drop the charges against him if he would provide them with "certain information." When the youth angrily refused, the agent waved a thick dossier at him. "Trying to break the American psychologically, the Russian read from reports about his finances, the financial condition of his parents, even about his life in the small town where he grew up." He was told that the file also contained fabricated charges of moral turpitude which the Russians would use to destroy his reputation in the United States."

When the American refused to be intimidated, the agent made the cruelest threat of all — against the young man's two-year old daughter whom he and his wife had left in the care of grandparents in the States. Stalling for time, the student said he would think it over and return. He went instead, to the U.S. Embassy and he and his wife were flown out of Russia.

A "parchment barrier"

One of the principal aims of the framers of the U.S. Constitution was to establish a legal and political system which would severely limit the government's power of surveillance. It is true that that noble document has become what Patrick Henry feared it would become if evil men were to occupy positions of power — "a parchment barrier against tyranny." Nevertheless, for two hundred years it held the secret agents and official spies at risk. Moreover, it is still the "supreme law of the land" and when the courts see fit to conform to its fundamental rules and principles, can bring to justice those functionaries who abuse their power.

Even so, successful prosecutions of government spies and "intrusion specialists" are rare. If the Watergate five had bugged a private home, officie or automobile, it is unlikely that they would ever have found themselves in court charged with a crime. Agents of the FBI, IRS, FDA and others daily commit worse offenses with impunity. The Watergate intruders had the misfortune to become involved in a political tong war that was to grow into the scandal of the century.

Former CIA operative E. Howard Hunt, who directed the Watergate caper, seemed a little puzzled that the same government which trained him for that kind of activity prosecuted him for using the skills they had taught him.

"Our Government trains people like myself to do these things," he told an interviewer. "It becomes a way of life for a person like me."

To justify the "way of life" in which Hunt was initiated early in his career, Government agency spokesmen cite overriding considerations such as national security, greater efficiency in combatting crime, especially the narcotics traffic; and prevention of civil disorders or violence.

"The ideal," a Defence Department security officer told Richard Harwood of the *Washington Post*, "is to eliminate risk in advance."

Another federal law-enforcement official stated the theory in more specific terms: "If someone is out there plotting a riot or a bombing, I think you will agree that it is better for society if we know about it and can act to head it off."[6]

The seductive element in this pleading is the implication that such methods will be used only against suspected criminals or terrorists.

The events of the past few years revealed with remarkable clarity that such is not the case. A system of espionage, once established, is applied first against that sector of society that is known to have criminal antecedents or to be closely linked to groups which have. Later, however, it is gradually extended to cover political foes, individuals who hold non-conformist views and, eventually, personal enemies of the power elite.

A striking example of the way in which this works may be seen in the history of the U.S. government's Organized Crime Drive.

The all-out war on organized crime was launched in the early 50s, after hearings before the Kefauver Senate subcommittee had revealed the extent to which crime syndicates had penetrated all levels of American society.

In 1961, immediately after taking over as Attorney General,

Robert F. Kennedy announced a sweeping plan to smash the operations of what he called the bankrollers and kingpins of the underworld. He was quoted as saying that there were "around a hundred" of these across the country.

Kennedy's basic programme called for pooling the efforts of all federal agencies which have investigative powers, such as the FBI, IRS, Drug Enforcement (then Bureau of Narcotics) and so on. When the drive got into high gear, some 26 of these agencies were funnelling information derived from clandestine surveillance into the files of the Justice Department.

Far from being limited to the estimated hundred "kingpins" and their associates, as promised by the Attorney General, the operation covered thousands of innocent citizens, who were subjected to covert intrusions into their private lives.

James E. Miggins, a former IRS special agent who had participated in the drive, later testified under oath that "anyone that has a bad reputation was put on the list, even though he was not a racketeer. Anyone in public office could be put on it also."[7]

Senator Edward V. Long, subcommittee chairman, summed up the situation in these words:

"It has been the testimony before this Committee that an agent can write to Washington and say, 'Put Mr. Smith on the OCD list,' and that's it. It is just a matter of someone's opinion. No jury says a man is guilty and is OCD."

Theory of pre-criminal intervention

Organized crime, however, remains one of the important arguments used to justify the imposition of a spy system that is inimical to and destructive of fundamental liberty.

The theory of what is called pre-criminal intervention, upon which such a system is based, has been treated at some length in the official publication of Interpol.

In part three of a series of articles entitled *Predelictual Action* published in Interpol's confidentially circulated organ, S. C. Versele, a Brussels jurist, lists the kinds of "dangerous persons" who should be singled out for special attention. Among those named were alcoholics, pimps, aggressive persons, vagrants, homosexuals, "immoral persons" ("their dangerousness is sometimes disguised under the mantle of 'liberty' and 'art' "); faith healers and prophets of new religions.[8]

With respect to the last two categories, it should be remarked that both contravene the oft-repeated Interpol declaration that:

"In affairs involving politics, religion, or race, Interpol becomes deaf and dumb."

The catch here is that there exists no universally accepted legal definition of religion. In America, for example, spiritual healing (the laying on of hands, "silent treatment," etc.), is fully acknowledged to be a legitimate part of religious practice; but to M. Versele persons who engage in such interventions are "clever confidence men," that is, criminals.

Russian satellite members of Interpol, being doctrinaire Marxists, regard all religion as "the opium of the people." Militant atheism is an important part of the official ideology. Moreover, Communist authorities often engage in persecution of religious believers under the guise of punishing secular crimes. For example, a Russian Jewish baker was tried, convicted and sentenced to prison for the "crime" of baking unleavened bread for the Jewish Passover. His criminal record shows only that he was found guilty of stealing state property, i.e., flour.

Political dissidents are often falsely charged with committing crimes that could identify them in Interpol files as wanted felons. If they succeed in escaping from their country, they can be labeled fugitives from justice rather than political refugees.

Just such a case was, in fact, responsible for J. Edgar Hoover's personal withdrawal from Interpol in 1950. The FBI chief, a bitter foe of Communism, resigned when ten Czechoslavakians escaped from their country and fled into West Germany, where they asked for political asylum. At the request of Czechoslavakia's Communist government, Interpol circularized the refugees as wanted criminals.

At the time the incident occurred, Hoover made it clear that he considered the Interpol action an abuse of that organization's proper function. He expressed his concern that it was opening the door to the future exploitation of Interpol by Russian satellite members for political ends.

Even after his resignation, Hoover, who had been an early enthusiast in the reorganization of Interpol in 1946, continued to make available to selected National Bureaus of the organization the FBI fingerprint files. Today, through the NCB in Washington and the Paris Secretariart, the files are accessible to all 122 member states.

In 1959, when a bill was pending in Congress to authorize the Treasury Department "and other agencies of the Government" to participate in Interpol, the FBI falsely stated:

"In 1950, the FBI withdrew its membership because the nature of its own activities permitted it to take advantage of very few of the benefits offered by Interpol."[9]

In the ensuing chapters, we will examine the history (including heretofore carefully veiled segments) and structure of Interpol. Later, we will see what can be learned from documented case histories involving an exchange of surveillance data between U.S. agencies and the international organization.

> *"The accretion of dangerous power does not come in a day; it does come, however slowly, from the generative force of unchecked disregard of the restrictions that fence in even the most disinterested assertion of authority."*
>
> — Justice Felix Frankfurter

3. *Accretion of Dangerous Power*

It will probably come as a surprise to most readers to learn that the word police, as applied to a law-enforcement agency, was unknown in England and America prior to the 19th century.

Up until that time, the job of maintaining public order belonged to the office of constable, or "guardian of the King's peace." The name derives from *comes stabuli* — master of the King's stables.

The term police was used generally to denote the department of government concerned with street lighting, sanitation and scaveging. Refuse collected from towns and sold to farmers to be used as fertilizer was known as "police manure."

(In the U.S. armed forces, even today, servicemen still speak of KP or "Kitchen police," and "policing up" to refer to cleaning and sanitation duties.)

The idea of a police force as a body of paid officers empowered to exercise surveillance over the population and to compel uniform obedience to official decrees, was introduced from France.

Writing in the August 12, 1756 issue of the magazine *World*, Lord Chesterfield observed that:

"We are accused by the French of having no word in our language which answers to their word *police*, which therefore we have been obliged to adopt, not having as they say, the thing."

In France, the *gendarmerie* had developed into an espionage system of frightening demensions. Louis XIV set up a network of secret agents who supplied him with endless reports about the private lives of his subjects. The King then summarily ordered the imprisonment of persons he believed guilty of some offence, even though there was not sufficient evidence to have them tried in court. It has been said that at one time one fourth of all the housemaids and servitors in Paris were paid informers for the police.

Philip Thicknesse, an English writer who, in 1797, produced a little book of useful hints for travellers planning to tour France, reported:

"The inteior police of Paris is very astonishing; nor can I leave this town and spend one night in any house at Paris, though no questions are asked me at the entrance, but the lieutenent of police has my name and my abode the next morning in his book, and most likely knows the business on which I went."[1]

In 1829 the British Parliament enacted legislation creating a permanent force of metropolitan police under Sir Robert Peel.

Not long afterward, a similar corps was established in New York. For the first time, a body of paid officers known as police and employed by the government to maintain a watch over the populace, became familiar to the English-speaking peoples.

During the initial years of their existence, the police in London had a difficult time of it. The whole idea was abhorrent to a large majority of Englishmen, who viewed the newly created force as an intolerable encroachment upon their liberty. Mobs rioted through the streets, carrying banners reading: "Down with the new police!" "Down with Peel's gang!"

The London *Standard* of November 9, 1830 took the side of the protesters:

"The police are unpopular and we should dispair of the spirit of Englishmen if an establishment so repugnant to the fundamental principle of the Constitution were not unpopular."

Despite its hostile reception, the metropolitan police force became permanently integrated into the English legal system. This was due in part to the fact that the Peelers, as they were called, demonstrated courage and efficiency in putting down crime, which was rampant and steadily growing worse.

Another factor responsible for bringing about the cautious acceptance of the police by the public was the untiring efforts of Commissioner Richard Mayne to establish good community relations.

Although Sir Robert Peel had laid the foundation for a police records system when the Metropolitan Police were created in 1829, only limited files were maintained during the ensuing forty years. But in 1869 the Parliament passed a bill known as the Habitual Criminal Act, requiring the police to keep a registry of convicted offenders.

By the turn of the century, central filing and dissemination of information on crime and criminals had become an important part of police duties.

Identification, too, had come to be a matter of considerable interest to the police, both in England and on the Continent. In France, the criminologist Alphonse Bertillon had introduced a system of identifying suspects by measurements of the body, head and limbs. His method required a record of 11 measurements to be taken on every criminal or suspicious person.

For a number of years thereafter, Bertillon's anthropometric technique was widely used by the police of many countries.

In England meanwhile, Chief Commissioner Edward Henry of Scotland Yard had established a simpler method of identification based upon fingerprint classification. Using a formulation worked out by the British eugenicist Sir Francis Galton, the Commissioner created a central fingerprint file and began to collect the prints of all known criminals in England.

The Galton-Henry system proved to be such an improvement over the Bertillon method, that in 1901 Henry invited leading criminologists and police officials from all over the world to a meeting in London to examine the new system in operation.

It is generally agreed that the London conference thus convened, marked the first move towards forming an organization for the purpose of international cooperation among criminal police forces.

It was not until 1914, however, that the "First International Congress of Criminal Police" was held. In that fatal year, with the advancing shadow of World War I less than three months away, police representatives from most of the Continental countries met in Monaco. The announced objective of the meeting was "to discuss plans for working together against the bands of international criminals who operate now in one country, now in another, and are easily able to elude the police with the help of modern methods of travel."

The conferees did little more than pass resolutions (at least, during their working sessions); but the proposals brought forward present a general outline of the organizational features eventually adopted in the formation of Interpol.

One of the problems recognized by those attending the Congresss was that of keeping the enormous number of international records within workable limits. As one observer at the meetings pointed out, it was not beyond human ingenuity (even in that pre-computer age) to work a registry containing as many as a million and a half records. The hitch was that the process of conducting searches among such massive files would be complicated and costly.

It was noted that even at that early date Scotland Yard had already compiled 200,000 files. If only a quarter of these were sent to the international central bureau, and other countries contributed in proportion, the resulting accumulation would be unmanageable.

Unlike the United States which enjoyed geographic isolation, European countries were small and contiguous. A "travelling criminal" as he was then called, might cross several international borders in the course of a single day's journey.

The conference ended on an optimistic note, with expressions of satisfaction at what had been accomplished and the announcement that the second international congress would be held in Bucharest two years later. In the interim, Monaco was to convene an international meeting in Paris to devise standardized identity cards based upon a combination of both the Bertillon and Galton-Henry systems.

Almost all countries except France and Holland had adopted the simpler fingerprint system but France stubbornly clung to the anthropometric method. After all, it had been invented by a Frenchman; and on the practical side, there was the problem of discarding thousands of records already collected, if they changed over to the fingerprint classification.

As it turned out, the initial meeting in Monaco kindled

more optimism than the international situation at the very moment justified. While Europe's policemen were trying to devise some means of dealing with counterfeiters, jewel thieves and confidence men, bigger malefactors were plotting a far greater crime against humanity.

Second Congress in Vienna

It was not until 1923, in fact, that the promoters of the Interpol idea felt enough solid ground under their feet to organize a second congress of police authorities and criminologists from all over the world.

Dr. Johannes Schober, Autrian State Chancellor and former police chief of Vienna, wrote to the heads of police departments in Europe, the U.S. and Latin America inviting them to attend an International Police Congress to be held in Vienna from September 3 to 6, 1923. He said the purpose of the convention would be to discuss the many difficulties the police authorities of all civilized nations have to overcome in the performance of their important work.

The problem of the international criminal had become more acute after the war. It was the age of the "roaring twenties." As always happens during and immediately following major armed conflicts, immorality, greed and vice had spread through the broad middle-class segment of society. Added to this was the alarming increase in drug addiction and alcoholism. Serious crimes such as murder, rape and armed robbery had grown to such proportions that the authorities of large cities were finding it impossible to cope with them.

Against this background, with its shifting population and imporved means of travel available to lawbreakers, the suggestion that law-enforcement agencies collaborate on an international level, had considerable appeal.

The Vienna meeting was attended by 120 delegates from 20 countries, representing all continents except Australia.[2]

The principal aim of the assembly was to draft a plan of action whereby the conferees would, upon their return home, try to persuade their respective governments to officially recognize the International Police Commission (IKK).

Although the United States and Britain were represented at the conference only by unofficial observers, some of the resolutions passed obviously were intended to encourage those countries to become active members of the international organization.

One of these proposals, adopted unanimously, concerned "flying warrants of arrest." It was agreed that in cases involving requests for arrest, no action would be taken by agents in those countries which forbids arrest or search without warrant, until such a warrant had been issued and application made for extradition. At the same time, it was agreed that in cases of serious crime, where it was not feasible to wait for the warrant and extradition request, a suspect would be detained for a given period of time to allow for the warrant to arrive.

During the course of their discussions, he delegates considered the following ideas, which indicate the trend of thinking from the outset of the organization's history:

— A suggestion that all countries establish the post of police attaché at their embassies on the same level with commercial, military and press attachés. (There are today, in fact, law-enforcement officials attached to all U.S., Russian and some British embassies; but many of them are officially listed as diplomats.)

— A proposal that an international police bureau be established within the League of Nations, attached to the Secretariat, or "if the appropriate moment for such an action has not come, an independent bureau with close ties to the League. (The contemporary Interpol has tried consistently during the past few years to gain official sponsorship of the

United Nation. Interpol's U.S. bureau falsely claimed in the memorandum submitted to Sen. Montoya — already cited — that the organization was in fact, under U.N. sponsorship.)

— An idea put forward by Dr. Oscar Dressler of the Austrian police, that Latin (which had served police in Europe as a *lingua franca* up to recent time) be adopted as a common international language. His suggestion was vetoed by the assembly, which chose instead English, French and German. Two resolutions submitted by the French delegate, M. Francois Renaut, one proposing that police of the various countries notify each other of the titles of censored movie films; the other suggesting that the sale of guns and issue of arms permits to youths under 18 be prohibited. Both propositions were adopted.

The delegates agreed that Vienna would become the permanent seat of the Commission. They gladly accepted Austria's offer to pay the costs of running the organization for the next five years. After 1928, the member countries were to pay one Swiss franc for each 10,000 of their population.

During the ensuing decade, the Commission held annual assemblies in various national capitals, including Berlin, Amsterdam, Antwerp, Paris, Rome and, of course, Vienna. The United States did not send official delegates to any of these meetings; but several American chiefs of police and judicial authorities apparently attended as informal observers.

At the congress held in Antwerp in 1930, it was decided to limit the international "wanted" circulations to ordinary criminal cases. This resolution was reaffirmed in both the constitution of 1948 and that adopted in 1956. Just how well Interpol has observed that stricture will become apparent in later pages of the present work.

On 17 April 1935 the Austrian minister sent a letter to the U.S. Secretary of State, formally inviting an official delegation from America to attend the Interpol congress to be held later that year in Copenhagen. The Secretary passed the request on to the Attorney General, asking his views as to the desirability of accepting.

According to a news report covering the Vienna convention, an agent of the FBI is mentioned among those present, but it is not known whether he represented the Government or J. Edgar Hoover who, said Attorney General Stanley Reed, "is already familiar with the work of the International Criminal Police Commission."

The following year, once again the Minister of Austria formally invited official U.S. participation in the 12th annual ICPC convention, to be held in Belgrade, Yugoslavia. Again, the State Department sought the advice of the Attorney General (at that time, Homer Cummings).

Secretary Cummings replied that his Department, "as well as the Director of the Federal Bureau of Investigation," had received previous correspondence from both the Interpol general secretary and police commissioner Kristian Welhaven of Oslo, Norway, urging that representatives of the FBI attend the meeting.

The Attorney General added that while J. Edgar Hoover would be unable to attend the congress, he thought it advisable to appoint an official from the American Legation or Consulate in Belgrade to represent the United States.

In a report submitted to the U.S. State Department by vice-consul John L. Calnan, who attended the conference, the American delegate offered the opinion that "this meetings brought forth nothing that is not already known to the American police, and that the principal reason for these meeting is to bring together chiefs of the various criminal police of the world for the purpose of making them personally acquainted with each other with a view to fostering an *esprit de corps* . . ."

Calnan's memorandum noted in passing that Germany was among the countries sending the largest delegations; but he did not remark on the Nazi character of the German conferees, nor their aggressive role in the assembly's discussions. He did mention that Lt. Gen. Deluege, director of Berlin's regional police (later hanged as a war criminal at Prague) rose to state his opposition to a resolution suggesting that a special committee for suppression of prostitution be formed and placed under the direction of the League of Nations. Deluege stated flatly that he could not agree with any system which would be controlled by the League of Nations.

His colleagues duly modified the proposal and agreed that all information pertaining to persons suspected or actually known to be engaged in traffic of women and children should be forwarded to Interpol's central bureau in Vienna.

Pressure on U.S. to Join

Interpol's campaign to persuade the U.S. to become a full-fledged member of the organization continued. In 1937 the host country for the ICPC world congress was Great Britain. Accordingly, the British Secretary of State for Foreign Affairs wrote a long letter to his opposite number in Washington, inviting the U.S. Government to send official representatives to the meeting.

To reassure the Americans that important things would be accomplished by the assembly, the Foreign Secretary noted that while there had been a tendency at past conventions to give undue prominence to the social side of the gatherings, "His Majesty's Government consider that an effort should be made to remedy this state of affairs, and that, in particular, the scale of entertainment of the delegates should be substantially reduced."

This was the kind of talk calculated to please the strong man of U.S. law-enforcement, J. Edgar Hoover, who sternly disapproved of policemen publicly behaving like boisterous bacchanates.

The FBI chief responded to the British invitation by appointing Assistant Director W.H. Drane Lester as official U.S. representative at the congress.

For reasons not clear at this date, Secretary of State Cordell Hull sought and obtained approval for the Lester appointment from President Roosevelt. In a letter transmitting Lester's certificate of designation, the Assistant Secretary of State informed the FBI agent that "in the absence of specific instructions from the Secretary of State, you are not authorized to enter into any oral or written agreement which may be construed as committing this Government to any definite course of action."

Another restriction on delegates imposed by the U.K. hosts, must have been regarded by Interpol Berlin as a direct slap at German members of the organization:

"His Majesty's Government consider that it is inappropriate that uniforms should be worn at a meeting of this character and it is consequently their desire that uniforms shall not be worn either at the various sessions of the meeting or at the official dinner."

At the Copenhagen meeting the previous year, General Deluege, — "a young, gay and arrant Nazi" — had appeared like a Hollywood star arriving at a premier showing of his latest film. Smartly attired in a bemedalled Lt. General's uniform of the Wehrmacht, he stepped jauntily from a big Mercedes sports car and strode into the assembly hall, followed by an aide-de-camp.

The no-uniforms rule at the London gathering did not greatly perturb the Nazi contingent, however. They had already planned to boycott the meeting. Captured war documents recently uncovered by researchers of the National Commission on Law Enforcement and Social Justice, reveal that the Germans had laid plans for an international police conference of their own, to be held in Berlin. Invitations were secretly extended to various countries that were bound to

Germany by police treaties, requesting the attendance of their representatives. More than a dozen countries sent delegates.

The Nazis were well aware (as is the Russian KGB today) that an international police organization can provide an ideal foreign intelligence network. They had hatched a scheme for using the police of Europe as "a counter-intelligence ideological front to combat Bolshevik infiltrations."

Full implimentation of the plan came in 1938, when Hitler's troops marched into Austria, and Interpol's central bureau and master files were taken over by Himmler's coldy efficient police chief, Reinhard Heydrich.

FBI man W.H. Drane Lester apparently could not foresee this, even in June 1937 — just nine months before it happened. In his confidential report to J. Edgar Hoover following the London conference, he recommended that the U.S. become a full-fledged, permanent member of Interpol. He suggested that the Attorney General select a delegate every year to attend the organization's congresses. Citing the strong interest shown by Interpol's members in the U.S. becoming a full participant, Lester said he had been informed that "any reasonable amount" would be acceptable as annual dues.

Acting upon the recommendation of FBI Director Hoover, Congress passed a bill on June 10, 1938 authorizing U.S. membership in the International Criminal Police Commission "and to incur the necessary expenses therefor, not to exceed $1,500 per annum."

At the time the measure was being deliberated, Congressmen were assured by its backers that activities of the International Police Commission would not in any manner affect that nation's diplomatic relations or political matters, "but are restricted solely to the exchange of information relative to technical and scientific methods of crime detection."

At the outset, this reassurance regarding Interpol's function must be measured against the fact that at the very time Congress approved membership, the Nazis had taken control of the Interpol nerve center in Vienna.

In fact, just ten days before the bill was passed, the U.S. had declined an invitation to send an American delgation to Interpol's 14th annual session in Rumania.

An "agreeable madness"

Predictably, there was a charged atmosphere at the 1938 gathering in Bucharest. By that time, even the most optimistic delegates from neutral countries sensed that the world was teetering on the edge of the abyss.

The representatives of Nazi Germany, led by Reinhard Heydrich, had come to the meeting with well-laid plans to take full control of the organization.

Those countries who would be allies in the coming war against the Axis powers fully recognized the Nazi cabal and countered by proposing that the seat of Interpol, now under the shadow of the swastika, be transferred from Vienna to some neutral country.

The motion was defeated by the general assembly.

To effect a "reconciliation among the 1938 convention's contending parties," the chief of Rumania's all-powerful secret police took the guests for a week-long dream cruise up and down the Danube aboard King Carol's royal yacht. Harry Soderman, head of Interpol Stockholm, recalls the excursion in these words:

"At every meal, Russian caviar was served in unlimited quantities. Champagne flowed from breakfast until late at night, beautiful gypsy singers sang melodious Transylvanian songs at all times. A bar, stocked to provide all the drinks of the entire world, was open free of charge twenty-four hours a day, and two orchestras played within earshot. In the evenings when we arrived at small fishing towns, all of the fishermen were out in their boats. Hundreds of them surrounded the ship, and in each boat there was a paper lantern and a man playing a mandolin. The effect of this on a dark night to one standing on a ship's bridge overlooking the black waters of the Danube, was enchanting.

"After a few days, one fell into a sort of agreeable madness. For my part, I was flirting with Maria Tarasana, the famous gypsy singer, with the Chief of Police of Hungary as my rival. Maria told us both that she would favor the one who danced the best Wallachian folk dances, so he and I spent several delightful nights trying to learn those difficult solo dances under her supervision. But clear up to the end of the voyage she was never able to decide which of us was the better dancer."

So much for Interpol activities which, U.S. Congressmen had been assured, "are restricted solely to the exchange of information relative to technical and scientific methods of crime detection."[3]

Whether Heydrich and his Rumanian allies were able to accomplish with champagne, caviar and gypsy girls what they had failed to accomplish in the assembly hall must be left to speculation. Soderman's account seems to imply that, for the time being at least, they succeeded. Amidst cordial farewells and well-wishers, the delegates parted, having agreed to meet the following year in Berlin.

In the formal invitation extended to the U.S. through the German Embassy in Washington, the purpose of the 1939 convention was described as "developing further and rendering still more successful the cooperation of the criminal police in the domain of the international war on crime."

The provisional programme, billed as a "day of experts," noted that the Berlin conference was being held "under the patronage of the Reichsführer SS and Chief of the German Police Heinrich Himmler."

Also invited to the 15th Session were members of the International Police Radio Technical Committee.

Even though Interpol had by this time fallen completely under Nazi control, the U.S. did not withdraw its membership. In declining the Third Reich's invitation, the American Government carefully avoided any reference to the take-over of the organization by Hitler's notorious secret police. Instead, the State Department reply said merely that "the advice and recommendations of the appropriate officials which have been received indicate that it will not be practicable for the Government of the United States to participate in the conference . . ."

In any case, the convention was never held. At the scheduled time, the "experts" were very busy with more pressing affairs; on September 1 of that year, Hitler's panzer columns roared into Poland, and the first blitzkrieg of the war was unleashed.

On the 8th December 1941 (the day following Pearl Harbor) Interpol members were given notice that the organization, which had been run by Reinhard Heydrich since 1940, was being transferred "with all its permanent administrative machinery," from Vienna to No. 16 am-Kleinen in Wansee, a suburb of Berlin.

There it was housed in Amt V of the Reich Main Security Office (RSHA), where it was combined with the Gestapo, criminal police and the SD, or secret security force.

"Under its new German leadership," Heydrich announced, "the ICPC will be a real world center of criminal police."

That could well be an accurate statement depending upon what is meant by the term, "criminal police."

> *"Nazism appears as the sign heralding the*
> *terrors of the year 2000."*
> — Jean-Michel Angebert

4. *Interpol Under Nazi Control*

During the Watergate uproar and its aftermath, "cover-up" came to be a familiar term. It has been assigned a permanent place in the political lexicon of our day, meaning the conceal-ment of information which might damage the reputation of a public figure, group, or government agency.

If the expression is contemporary, however, the thing it designates — the subtle art of whitewash — is as old as public opinion. As the history of ancient civilizations clearly shows, it was flourishing in the civil life of the earliest States. In the Athens of 500 B.C., it had become the common practice of successful lawyers, demagogues and office holders.

The Romans not only adopted the technique, but improved upon it through legal sophistry and the "source credibility" of great orators like Cicero and Quintillian.

In our time, we have seen added to these venerable sleights of hand, the persuasive know-how of a vast army of image-makers, working through the various media. Virtually every branch of the federal government has its own public relations office, whose "information specialists" are busy churning out news releases, memoranda, official statements, denials or corrections of published stories, and so on. Some of these are factual; some haven't enough truth in them to stain litmus paper.

But let us come to the case at bar — the wartime history of Interpol.

The U.S. Treasury's official memorandum, *Facts Concerning Interpol*, states:

"Certain allegations have been made that Interpol was part of the Nazi Gestapo during World Warr II. The International Criminal Police Commission commenced operation in 1923, and was located in Vienna, Austria until 1942 under Austrian Minister Dressler as Secretary General. Interpol's normal activities continued from 1923-1938, at which time German forces occupied Austria.

"From that moment other countries ceased cooperating, and Interpol activities rapidly became non-existent." (Emphasis added).

These "facts," although boldly asserted, do not correspond to documented history. An official report by the Allied Control Authority, Office of the Military Government, which took over when Germany surrendered, affirms that:

"In 1941, the files and staff were removed [from Vienna] to No. 16 am Kleinen, Berlin-Wansee and installed in a large house. There the files were re-indexed and a new folder system installed. Operations were continued right up to the end of the war. The final number of the magazine was dated 20 February 1945.

"The testimony of a former employee indicates that the IKPK [German abbreviation for Interpol] had a staff of between 15 and 20 persons for its Berlin operations.

"It was connected to a teletype network and was well supplied with telephone service.

"Photographs found on the premises indicate that much had been done to impress visiting police authorities with the plant and the operations of the IKPK. The building had been completely equipped and sumptuously furnished."

Some 18 countries — German satellites and neutral nations — remained dues-paying members of Interpol throughout the war.[1] While no official congresses were held, "the IKPK apparently tried to maintain international contacts and implications to the end." These contacts were directly between police authorities of the various member countries and through the exchange of information by radio and correspondence.

Curiously enough, the Allied Control Authority memorandum also notes that in 1942 the FBI was still carried in an Interpol report as a cooperating agency.

Interpol apologists, faced with indisputable evidence of the organization's wartime activity under Nazi control, assert that what happened in Europe thirty years ago is irrelevant so far as today's "re-constituted" Interpol is concerned.

(It is noteworthy that those who keep permanent files linking individuals with their past, — files in which nothing is ever forgotten, nothing forgiven — believe that a criminal chapter in the history of their own organization ought to be expunged because "it happened so long ago.")

Even so, their argument would have some merit except for one fact of paramount importance. It is this:

A continuity of personnel, policy, and records can be traced from the present Interpol operation directly back to that vast concentration of despotic power known as the Sicherheitsdienst (SD) in the Berlin suburb of Wansee.

Several members of the committee which reorganized Interpol after the collapse of the Third Reich had either worked under or cooperated with the Nazi-run system during the war. Four out of seven of Interpol's presidents since its restructuring in 1946 may reasonably be considered carriers of the police-state germ. Incredibly, one of the more recent heads of the organization was a former SS officer who had served with the dreaded SD, the Security Service under the direction of the notorious Reinhard Heydrich. In the hands of the latter, according to an allied counter-intelligence report, "the SD grew into a highly efficient political intelligence system and later became the most effective instrument for suppression at the disposal of the Nazi regime."[2]

A dubious past

It is certainly reasonable to ask: if the post-war Interpol was to function in a manner acceptable to the free world, why did its organizers choose executives who had — at best — a dubious past? Why did they not display the common sense embodied in the Spanish proverb — "For thy vineyard, take the cutting from a good vine."?

Former agents and collaborators who had operated the mechanisms of Nazi tyranny were not qualified to direct a global police apparatus linked to democratic systems, unless —

Unless it was to be a new model of the same machine, that required their experience and expertise in its operation.

Or perhaps the motivation is to be found in the supranational esprit de corps of the police fraternity which, like the world's intelligence services, seems to recognize no national boundaries.

Whatever the rationale, Interpol's rebuilders did not act out of innocence. Their later attempts, first to conceal, and then to fumigate the record is proof of that.

Official spokesmen for Interpol — whether in Washington, Paris or London — who insist that critics are over-reacting to the situation have nevertheless been at some pains to deny or to misrepresent the facts.

A compelling illustration of this point is the case already alluded to, of former SS officer Paul Dickopf, who was Interpol president from 1968 to 1972.

Even after researchers in 1973 had uncovered documents among Nazi war records which established beyond dispute Dickopf's service in the SS, Interpol spokesmen sought to euphemize and soft-pedal the issue. The statement prepared by Interpol's U.S. bureau for distribution to inquiring Senators and curious Congressmen put it this way:

"Allegations have also been made that Mr. Paul Dickopf, the President of Interpol from 1968-1972, was a former Nazi SS Officer . . .

"Early in October of 1939, after the campaign against Poland he was *automatically enrolled* in the General SS as an SS Untersturm führer [Lieutenant] because of the Police Commissioner rank he had held." (Emphasis added.)

With Dickopf's SS personnel file and serial number (SS-337259) at hand, it is hardly an *allegation* to affirm that he was a member of the nefarious corps of torturers, murders and Jew-liquidators.

Furthermore, the assertion that Dickopf was automatically enrolled in the innermost circle of the Nazi system of concentric elites, is absurd. Heinrich Himmler subjected each SS applicant to fanatical scrutiny. In a speech to the German General Staff in 1937, he declared:

"When I took over the SS, I had a racial idea in mind. The men I wanted were of Aryan blood. Sedulously, I studied their photographs for ethnological hints. If I found a man possibly Slavic, I discarded him. Thousands of pictures crossed my desk — and each of these I remember! I wanted an aristocracy of blood. I wanted the perfect German man and him multiplied a hundred thousand fold. These men I have found. They are the fathers of the new Germany."[3]

A candidate for SS enlistment had to prove an Aryan pedigree back to the year 1750. "Membership was strictly supervised on such factors as height, complexion, facial structure, etc."[4] When an SS man wished to marry, his prospective wife had to be investigated as well, and approved by the organization's top command.

As the Nazi Party's instrument of control, the black-uniformed troops spread terror throughout all Germany and German-occupied territories. It is important to bear in mind that, as one writer on the subject has reminded us, "the behaviour of each individual SS member, whatever his rank, typified the system and its basic orientation."[5]

The SS was not only Hitler's private army; it was also a mystique, a religion of race and blood. This is confirmed by the initiatory character of the Black Order's induction ceremonies. The French writer, Jacques Delarue states that "the swearing in of the young SS men took place at midnight, by the light of torches, in Brunswick Cathedral before the coffin containing the bones of Henry the Fowler."[6]

The elite formation's double SS designation was itself written as a runic sign, having an esoteric meaning that only the leaders could interpret correctly. Trevor-Roper was not indulging in journalistic hyperbole when he called Himmler "the terrible high-priest of Hitler."

The Bavarian chicken-raiser, who became the most sinister figure of the Nazi regime, was, like others in Hitler's entourage, a dabbler in the occult. He believed in "the more dubious theories of naturist eugenics, in the psychic virtues of natural diet," and in medieval herbalism. (He assigned prisoners in the concentration camps to grow special medicinal plants for his private use.)

But Himmler's lack of formal education and cultural refinement was scarcely a drawback in creating the kind of police-state system he was to impose upon the Third Reich. On the contrary, it was to his advantage and in keeping with the kind of character the Führer himself had spelled out for his standard-bearers:

"We shall encourage the growth of a violent, domineering, intrepid, cruel youth . . . I want it to have the strength and the beauty of young, wild animals."

To implement this cannon and to prepare young men for their terrifying duties, special schools for Führers (Führerschules) were established. For admission to one of these schools, the applicant had to have certain qualifications with respect to age, past employment, and Party loyalty, as shown by having served at least four years in the SA, SS or in the Hitlerjugend.

Positive attitude to Nazism

Paul Dickopf, who was trained at the Führerschule der Sicherheitspolizei in Berlin-Charlottenburg, had been a Nazi since 1933, when he joined the German Nationsocialist Student Organization. A good athlete, he had received a Sports Badge in recognition of his participation in sports activities of the SA (Hitler's original Brown Shirts, who were later supplanted by the SS.)

While never an outstanding student at the university (which he left before completing his studies), Dickopf had other qualifications that were more important to Obersturmbannführer [Lt. Col.] Otto Hellwig, the SD officer who checked his eligibility to enter the Führerschule. Chief among these were "marked willpower and personal hardness;" and "positive attitude to National Socialist ideology."

Academic prerequisites were minimal because the goals of the SS were not concerned with intellectual pursuits, but with brutal, naked force and the animal cunning, the sly arts of the secret agent, necessary to achieve them.

"These men sought only power — power over other men, over institutions, over Germany, over other nations, if possible over the world and the future. All was to go according to their will."[8]

(Let us add that while this statement accurately describes the motives and purposes of the SS in the Hitler era, it applies equally well to the Soviet KGB of today.)

Additional points covered in Dickopf's application include general racial picture (good); behavior on and outside of duty (correct); finances (in order); character qualities; degree of skill and training; sport; ideology; abilities and knowledge in the interior service, disciplinary administration and administration.

Summing up, the general assessment states: "Dickopf is, according to his character, posture, behavior and knowledge, a thoroughly suitable SS Führer."

Dickopf's file contains also a curriculum vitae in his own handwriting and bearing his signature. He says of himself (in translation):

"I was born on the 9th June 1910, son of the elementary school teacher Joseph Dickopf and his wife Elizabeth, neé Bellinger in Muschenbach, district Wiesbaden. I attended elementary school and high school [Realschule] in Wiesbaden-Biebrich, where I obtained the leaving certificate at Easter 1928.

"Originally, I wanted to become head forest ranger; however, due to the low number of situations, I had no access to this career. Therefore, to begin with, I studied two semesters of administration law at the University of Frankfurt a/M and another one in Vienna, and worked as a student who earns his living, at the foundry Gute-Hoffnung in . . .

"After two further semesters as guest listener at the University of Berlin, I interrupted my studies which, after further unsuccessful efforts to be admitted to a forest ranger school, I took up again in the summer of 1932 as a student of law at the University of Frankfurt.

"In 1934, as a member of the National Socialist German Student Organization, I took part in a course of the SA Sport school in Adelsheim, and then did a one-year voluntary army service at the 8. (MG) Kp. JR 20 (now 41) in Amberg, where I was discharged as corporal of the reserves and non-commissioned officer on the 12.10.1935.

"In the following two semesters, I was mainly occupied with civil-legal questions and problems of forensic chemistry, forensic medicine and psychology. After a six-weeks introductory period at the county court in Weisbaden and after passing the first examination of non-commissioned officers of the reserves, I applied for entry into the career of higher criminal officers.

"On the 1.6.37, I was employed as criminal commissar candidate at the head office of criminal police in Frankfurt. There I went through the various service offices and worked informatively with the county police, the Protective police, Administrative police, and lately, three months with the SD RFSS (Security Service of the Reichsführer of the SS), in the Fulda-Wesser district of Frankfurt/Main; and effective from 12th October 1938 until 1.7.1939, admitted to the 13th course of the Criminal Commissar Candidates of the Führerschule of the Security Police in Berlin-Charlottenburg.

"Prior to the seizure of power, I was not politically active. I became a member of the National Socialist German Student Organization on 13.5.33, to which I belonged until I entered the police. During that time I took part in various educative and instructive courses of the National Socialist [Nazi] German Student Organization in Frankfurt."

Paul Dickopf, president of Interpol from 1968 to 1972, was a former Nazi SS officer, who served with the dreaded SD, the intelligence and espionage arm of the elite corps.

Cover of Interpol's monthly publication pictures Reinhard Heydrich, notorious "Hangman of Poland," who was wartime president of the organization.

When Dickopf completed his training at the Führerschule in Charlottenburg, the commandant in charge and 15 officers held a meeting to determine whether he now qualified for a commission. After reviewing his record, they unanimously agreed that he did.

Accordingly, on 1 July 1939, Paul Dickopf was given the rank of Untersturmführer in a unit of the SD (the intelligence and espionage arm of the SS). The exact nature of his activities thereafter is not known. In his service file, opposite the sub-heading *Kind of Duty*, the information is illegible. This is not the only gap in the record. The entire contents of Section III are missing, as is a photograph from the top of his career document. Similarly, an enclosure sent with a notification document dated 23 November 1944 from the Karlsruhe AD Station has been removed. A later notation has been added: "There exists an arrest order at this time against the above mentioned, who is reported missing."

Secrecy was essential

Such lacunae and additions are hardly surprising if considered in the light of Dickopf's undercover work with the SD, and the laundered version of it to be circulated by Interpol at a later date.

Himmler's insistence upon secrecy was almost pathological. He had his own nephew, Hans Himmler, an SS lieutenant, sentenced to death for revealing SS secrets while drunk. The sentence was commuted to frontline service with a parachute division; but when the younger Himmler talked too much a second time, he was sent to the concentration camp at Dachau and liquidated there as a homosexual.

If exact details of Dickopf's duties are missing, however, the general nature of his job is well known. It involved total surveillance of everyone living under the rule of the Third Reich; information gathering; and what Eugen Kogan has aptly termed "the exercise of terror on a huge scale."

"Day by day, year after year, this far-flung intelligance network supplied a mass of individual reports from every sphere of life — the Party, the government, industry, high society, the private lives of ordinary citizens. Each report reached the central office, which kept one copy in its secret files, sending two copies to the chief of the SD administrative district concerned. One of these copies was kept in a file to which only this official and his deputy had access; the other in a place known to him alone."[9]

The avowed aim of Reinhard Heydrich, ruthless chief of the SD, was to bring every individual in the German sphere under continuous surveillance. He was a born intelligence officer, says Felix Kersten, "a living card index, a brain which held all the threads and wove them all together."[10]

In his history of the SS, *The Order of the Death's Head*, Heinz Hoenne corroborates this opinion. "Heydrich was ideally equipped to be head of a secret service — he was hard, he was unsentimental, his thirst for information was apparently insatiable, and his contempt for his fellowmen was enough to make the flesh creep."

Heydrich was indeed a figure whose mental and social make-up are not without clinical interest.

It has been said that history can provide few examples of psychoneurotic personalities to match that of this man. His cold intelligence; his code of behavior, devoid of even the most rudimentary moral sense; his single-minded lust for power as an end in itself — only a Caesar Borgia or a despot from the last days of the Roman Empire can be compared with him.

As a result, says Wilhelm Hoettl, who served under him, Heydrich's whole life was one long series of criminal enormities: murders of people whom he disliked, of opponents and those he regarded as untrustworthy.

He had an unhealthy preference for the company of prostitutes, whom he enlisted as informants in his vast system of espionage. In addition to the great number of such spies whom he had recruited during his frequent visits to the red light districts of Berlin, he established a luxuriously appointed brothel which operated directly under his control. It became widely known as the Kitty Salon and was staffed not only by the professional sisterhood but by girls from the best society, who volunteered for the work out of "patriotism."

These "faith and beauty girls," as they were called, were chosen not only for their charm and good looks, but for their cultural background, intelligence and knowledge of languages.

Bugs in the bedrooms

Heydrich's technical aides installed microphones in all the rooms of the house and in the most intimate nooks of the bar. These listening devices were connected to a listening post in the cellar.

Walter Schellenberg, whom Heydrich had detailed to set up the operation, later reported that it proved a great success in supplying the SD with intelligence data. The steady stream of important foreign diplomats, businessmen and office holders who frequented the establishment blabbed freely to their seductive companions of the evening.

In the manipulation of his highly developed system of dossiers to degrade or destroy important enemies, Heydrich sometimes inserted false data into the files, or deliberately confused identities. This was the method he used to ruin Gen. Werner von Fritsch, commander-in-chief of the German Army.

During routine investigation by the police, a veteran blackmailer named Otto Schmidt mentioned that among his victims had been an army officer named von Fritsch, whom he had observed in a homosexual act. All the details were carefully written out and the officer identified as General von Fritsch. The report was then passed on to Himmler, who laid it before Der Führer himself.

After a cursory look at the eight-page document, Hitler ordered Himmler to "burn this muck."

Heydrich duly had the Fritsch file destroyed, but not until he had carefully made extracts of the more salient particulars. Later, Goering, who was feuding with the General, ordered the Fritsch file reconstituted, and it was used to put an end to the career of the senior Werhmact officer.

It was subsequently learned that the blackmailer's testimony had, in fact, referred to a retired army captain named von Fritsch, whose data had been mixed with that of the General's file.

Another favorite method of bringing prominent people under Heydrich's control was to prove that they were not of pure Aryan descent.

One of the targets of his ancestral witch hunts was Dr. Robert Ley, the Reichsführer of the German Labour Front. In reviewing Ley's secret dossier, Heydrich discovered something in the leader's *adnenpapiere* (racial heredity certificates) which made him believe that Ley had Jewish antecedants.

To obtain documentary proof that would confirm his suspicions, Heydrich ordered his agents to burglarize the office of Walter Buch, Chief Justice of the Party, where Ley's personal file was kept.

The Ellsberg-type break-in did not produce the evidence he sought, but Heydrich continued his search and apparently used what he learned to his own advantage.

Not even Hitler, nor Heydrich's own boss, Himmler, escaped his passion for genealogical excavations. His secret file

on the Führer, which vanished after his assassination, reportedly contained, among other bits of derogatory information,
material purporting to show that Hitler himself was not ra-
cially pure.

Secret file on Himmler

As for Himmler, the first data on this subject were entered in
his secret dossier in 1933, when Heydrich learned that a
Jewish cattle dealer of Wuerttemberg had appeared at Munich
Police headquarters asking to see the new Chief of Police
Heinrich Himmler who, he claimed, was his cousin. The
matter was immediately referred to Himmler who, to the
amazement of his staff, ordered the man released, declaring
that he was not to be molested thereafter. The full story of
Himmler's connection with the non-Aryan was never disclosed, but was kept under seal in Heydrich's GRS (*Geheime
Reichssache* — State Secret) file.

Ironically, Heydrich's own lineage came under scrutiny
about the same time he was digging into that of Himmler and
other top-ranking figures of the German Reich.

A master baker of Halle, Heydrich's birthplace, told friends
that Heydrich's grandmother, Sara, whom he had known
personally, was a Jewess, who had married a gentile. This
would make Heydrich's father half-Jewish.

When the story reached the ears of Rudolf Jordan, the Party
Gauleiter for Halle-Merseburg, he wrote to Gregor Strasser,
Nazi Organization Chief, suggesting that the Personnel De-
partment investigate the rumor.

Heydrich immediately took the baker to court, charged
with slander. The case was quickly decided in the plaintiff's
favor, owing to the fact that the baker could not produce any
documentary evidence to support his reckless allegations.

When his lawyer tried to subpoena the pertinent page of the Marriage and Birth Registers from Halle, it was found that the entries for the month of March 1904 (Heydrich was born March 1904) were mysteriously missing.

According to Wilhelm Hoettl, the question of Heydrich's "Jewish Taint" arose twice again — in 1935 and 1937 — but neither case got as far as a public hearing in court. In one instance, the tattler formally retracted his assertion in a sworn statement; in the other, the offender "disappeared for good into a concentration camp."[11]

Hoettl adds that when Heydrich had assigned a trusted SS henchman to steal all the documents pertaining to his father's pedigree, he overlooked the fact that in a Leipzig cemetery was a tombstone bearing the name Sara Heydrich. When this one remaining link with his progenitors did occur to him, he ordered the same Sturmscharführer who had purloined the embarrassing records to deal with the matter.

One dark night the trusty SS Sargeant-Major removed the gravestone from the burial plot and heaved it into a near-by river. Heydrich had it replaced by another marker which carried a shorter, but less revealing, inscription: "S. Heydrich." The stonecutter's bill was found in Heydrich's personal office following the surrender of Germany in 1945.

Despite this suspected blemish on his own ancestral record (some psychologists say because of it), Heydrich master-minded that diabolical scheme for the mass extermination of Jews, known as the Final Solution. "It was he who invented the horrible machinery by which, 'in an imperceptible man-ner,' millions of people were hounded to their death."[12]

One of the fundamental features of Heydrich's plan, which, strikingly illustrates the fiendish cast of his mind, was that Jews would be employed in the work of annihilating other Jews.

To implement this scheme, the Security Police turned to their extensive files. From these they extracted a number of

Jews with criminal histories (whether real or false), whom they forced by blackmail and promises of material advantages to recruit others from the Jewish community to carry out the monstrous undertaking.

There can be no doubt that the Interpol files transferred from Vienna to Berlin by Heydrich in 1940 provided much of the data needed to carry out the satanic plot. In his history of the Gestapo, Jacques Delarue reports that "he obtained about five thousand men and women who, apart from the certainty of being spared, received a financial share of the pillage. They were charged with the extermination of their unfortunate co-religionists."

Heydrich's assurances of "being spared" were, of course, as perfidious as all his promises. He told members of his own circle that he was following the example of the Pharoahs of ancient Egypt who had put to death the workmen who constructed their tombs, so that their burial places would remain secret.

Dr. Simon Wiesenthal, noted postwar Nazi hunter, who helped track down Adolf Eichman, has confirmed the implication of war-time Interpol with Heydrich's genocide machinery.

In a letter dated 14 March 1975, to U.S. Rep. John E. Moss, Dr. Wiesenthal wrote that "the Conference of Wansee on January 20, 1942, where the decision was taken to exterminate the Jews of Europe, took place in the offices of Interpol. The headquarters of the Security Office (Reichssicherheits Hauptamt) made use of the files of Interpol to blackmail people or to make them work as spies for Germany."

He added the wise observation that it is always dangerous if a non-demoncratic regime gets hold of documents meant to serve the ends of justice . . . "They always use them for political purposes."

Four months after the Wansee Conference, Heydrich was

assassinated; but his mass-murder organization continued to function smoothly long after his death.

Successor to the "Hangman"

Himmler deliberated eight months over the problem of a successor to Heydrich. He wanted a Gestapo chief who could be capable of carrying on the hellish work his predecessor had begun, and with the same ruthless efficiency.

In late January 1943, he announced his choice. It was Ernst Kaltenbrunner, a fanatical Austrian Nazi and Lieutenant General of Police, whose chief distinction for Himmler was that he had successfully established an extensive intelligence network throughout his jurisdiction.

Physically, Kaltenbrunner was a giant, almost seven feet tall. His Herculean broad shoulders, thick neck and heavy movements gave an impression of immense strength and brutality. "A great flat forehead had nothing intellectual about it; a pair of small, brown hard eyes, glittering and deep-set and half covered by heavy lids; a big straight mouth like a slash, thin lips and a huge, thick square chin" further stressed the man's bestial aspect.

Schellenberg said of him that he looked at one fixedly, his eyes "like the eyes of a viper seeking to petrify its prey." He conducted any kind of interview like a interrogation; he would not immediately respond to a question or comment, but would remain impassive and staring. Then, after a brief interval of oppressive silence, he would bang the table and begin to talk.

Kaltenbrunner was a chronic alcoholic, whose drinking started with champagne and brandy when he arrived at his office in the morning and continued throughout the day. A chain smoker, he consumed five packs of cigarettes a day.

Heydrich had always tried to draw a veil of secrecy and

tight security around his diabolical operations, but Kaltenbrunner cast aside all camouflage and circumlocution. Now when department chiefs of the Reich Main Security Office met for discussion at regular luncheons, the technique of mass murder was openly, and at times jocularly, talked about.

During the war crimes trials at Nuremberg, Hans-Bernd Gisevius, a civil servant and secret anti-Nazi, testified that "the gruesome chapter of the installation of the first gas chamber was discussed in detail in this circle, as were the experiments as to how one could most quickly and most efficiently remove the Jew. These were the most horrible descriptions I have ever heard in my life."

Kaltenbrunner was not satisfied with mere discussions and reports, however. He personally inspected the death camps, a practice he had begun before he took over Heydrich's post. During a visit to the notorious Mauthausen concentration camp in 1942, he insisted upon observing first-hand how a group of prisoners were transported to the gas chamber, and thereafter watched their death agonies through a spy hole.

Soon after he became head of the German Security Service, Kaltenbrunner returned to Mauthausen, this time to witness the experimental killing of prisoners by three different methods, namely, by being shot in the neck, by gassing and by hanging. The executions were all carried out in his presence.

Camp employees and prisoners who survived the war later testified before the International Military Tribunal that Kaltenbrunner arrived at the camp in high spirits and laughed and joked throughout the experiments.

Such, then, was the man who was president of Interpol during the years 1943-1946. In a message to Interpol members, published in the organizations official organ of 10 June 1943, Kaltenbrunner said he was taking over presidential direction of the international police association because "it concerns a really great deal of culture in which I see, so to speak, a precious inheritance of my compatriot Schober."

He added that it was his sincerest aspiration to maintain the spirit of Interpol as already established and "to lead it into the future with a flourish."

Among the Interpol appointments he confirmed upon taking office was that of permanent reporter, assigned to his friend, Inspector General F. E. Louwage of the Belgian police.

Louwage was the member who initiated the reorganization of Interpol after the war.

Serving with Kaltenbrunner as Interpol's vice-president and director of the organization's International Bureau was SS-General Arthur Nebe.

At the time, Nebe — a veteran policeman and early joiner of the Nazi Party — was chief of the German Criminal Police. During his prior service as head of the Berlin Police, he had gained considerable repute as a criminologist and author of an authoritative treatise on police techniques.

Heydrich, who was always quick to spot the kind of talent he needed for his organization, had persuaded Nebe to join the German Security Service and to bring with him several of his subordinates to form a team of experts at the SD headquarters.

According to Wilhelm Hoettl, Nebe worked hand-in-glove with Heydrich and at no time repudiated his methods. On the contrary, "there was hardly an operation of any importance in which he did not play his part; and he did his utmost to foster and deserve the reputation of being one of Heydrich's trustworthy collaborators."

When Heydrich organized police commando units called *Einsatzgruppen* to follow the German troops as they advanced into Russia, Nebe volunteered to take command of one of the groups (Einsatgruppe B). These contingents, which have been called "a determined army of death," were formed by recruits from both the SS and from the ranks of regular police forces throughout the Third Reich. Their orders were to "act with ruthless energy" to seize and destroy all politically and racial enemy groups. That meant Bolsheviks, Jews, Gypsies and even prisoners of war. Regarding the latter, an official document declared: "The Bolshevik soldier has forfeited all right to be treated as an honourable foe, in the light of the Geneva Convention."

Evidence presented at the Nuremberg trials indicated that Group B, commanded by Nebe, was responsible for the savage massacre of at least 45,000 men, women and children in the space of five months.[13]

Despite this horrendous record, Harry Soderman, (Swedish criminologist who was one of the prime-movers in re-establishing Interpol after the war) characterizes Nebe as a "very mild Nazi." Of both Nebe and his deputy, Carlos Zindel, Soderman wrote:

"They and I were to become very close personal friends and I have always lamented their terrible ends."[14]

Certain writers have stated or implied that Nebe carried out Heydrich's demonic orders only under compulsion and that he was at heart an enemy of Nazism. This view is based on the fact that he was implicated in the Generals' plot against Hitler's life.

Plan for survival

The truth is that Nebe was an opportunist. He had no deep-rooted ideological convictions, but possessed a keen foresight with respect to political trends. He secretly joined the Nazi Party in 1932, while serving as a member of the Prussian Criminal Police because he sensed that "it was the party to which the future would belong; that this was a future lasting only a few years he did not at first foresee."[15]

When Nebe realized that the thousand year Reich would

not survive another thousand days, he cast about for an escape hatch. A friend whom he had known many years and who was an authenic member of the anti-Nazi underground, provided it for him.

Nebe had suspected for some time that one of his close friends — Dr. Hans-Bernd Gisevius, a government consultant — was involved in some way with the German resistance fighters. He shrewdly reasoned that with the final collapse of the shattered Third Reich, Gisevius would emerge as a person of influence in whatever post-war regime the Allies formed or allowed to be formed in Germany. Nebe could easily then seek and obtain an important position in the new police force that would have to be organized.

With this in mind, Nebe felt his way carefully into his friend's confidence and Gisevius eventually vouched for him to other members of the underground movement.

The cabal cautiously accepted Nebe because they thought that in his position he could be of considerable help as a highly placed intelligence source.

As it turned out, however, the amount of really useful information he passed on to opposition leaders was scant indeed.

Moreover, Nebe's role in the 20th July Plot, according to Gestapo agents who conducted the subsequent investigation, was at best a peripheral one.

It has been said that Kaltenbrunner did not have the slightest suspicion that his deputy was in any way connected with the conspiracy. Nebe would have survived the bloody purge which followed if he had not panicked and fled.

It has never been clearly established what happened to Nebe following his getaway. Some researchers have reported that he was caught by the Gestapo and strangled in several agonizing stages with a noose of piano-wire; others that he made good his escape and joined the lost legion of other Nazi criminals who were never heard of again.

As noted earlier, Kaltenbrunner was hanged as a war criminal in 1946.

We have briefly reviewed the character and some of the typical deeds of these top executives of the wartime Interpol for two reasons.

First, the impact of their personalities, methods and records is still to be found (in carefully screened ways) in the current operations of that organization.

Second, they are pertinent to the question regarding the Nazi background of an Interpol President in our own day, that is, ex-SS officer Paul Dickopf. For, if we are to believe documentary proof as well as the words of Himmler's closest associates, he expected in every member of his SD "all the virtues implicit in his sacred order."

These "virtues" were, first and foremost, blind obedience, and maximum efficiency in setting up and operating the machinery of espionage and terror that represents the logical and inevitable culmination of all systems of spy government.

> *"The curse of a system of terror is that there is no turning back; neither in the large realm of policies nor the smaller realm of human relationships."*
>
> — Hans Bernd Gisevius

5. *Twilight Of The Beasts*

The final months of World War II were a period of frantic activity for leaders of the SS, and the German intelligence services.

It was clear, even to the most die-hard Nazis among them, that *der Tag* was at hand. Personal survival was at stake; it was every fox his own tail. Individually and in small groups, the guilty sought ways to eradicate all traces of their crimes and to lay plans for a postwar incarnation as loyal, but respectable Germans, ready to resume their customary places in civilian life.

An important question which occupied their attention was what to do with the extensive files and records which had been compiled and maintained with Teutonic thoroughness. It was necessary, they felt, to preserve the bulk of them for continued use in a reorganized police system after the war. Those which might incriminate SS officers or prove embarrassing in other ways, had to be altered or destroyed.

As early as the 31 January, 1945, a large-scale removal of records, not only from secret police archives but from other government agencies as well, had begun. Gestapo files were moved from the Berlin headquarters to Munich, and those found likely to be prejudicial in the eyes of Allied victors, were burned.

Later, as the Allied armies advanced deeper into Germany, and the fall of Berlin was imminent, thousands of SS men began a retreat toward the region known as the Alpine Redoubt in the heart of the Austrian Alps. This natural defense area had originally been planned as a final fortress where the remnants of the wehrmacht could keep enemy forces at bay while their generals negotiated a peace settlement with the British and Americans who, they thought, would then turn on the Soviet troops and drive them back into Russia.

Work had actually begun on fortifying the mountain strong-hold, but it had to be abandoned because the builders found that they had neither sufficient materials nor manpower to complete it intime to be of use.

The district was still regarded as the best place to seek cover from the firepower of the invading armies. It was also the safest spot to hide documents and treasure. According to Simon Wiesenthal, the senior officers of the SD chose the area as a cache for their secret papers.

SS Colonel Karl Zindel loaded a car with Interpol files and fled southward from Wansee, apparently heading for Switzerland. He was stopped at Stuttgart by French troops who, after identifying him, contemptuously dismissed him with an order to report later the same day at an interrogation cage to be processed as a prisoner of war.

Humiliated and fearful of the punishment he knew would be meted out to him for his war crimes, Zindel went to a park and committed suicide by swallowing potassium cyanide.

The part of Interpol files he was transporting thus came into possession of the French. Zindel's superior, Ernst Kaltenbrunner, had earlier sent another of his deputies — Wilhelm Hoettl — to Switzerland to offer Allen Dulles, U.S. intelligence chief, the surrender of Austria, where the archives and, it is said, a vast Nazi treasure was concealed.

The strategem was unsuccessful, and Kaltenbrunner was caught trying to "dive under" in Southern Germany. He had shaved his mustache in the vain hope that it would alter his appearance enough for him to escape through Allied lines. Accompanying him was his mistress, Countess Gisella von Westrop.

Kaltenbrunner's getaway luggage contained no confidential papers; but was bulging with counterfeit banknotes in US dollars and British pounds; an assortment of chocolate, candy and liquor bonbons; stolen jewelry; and several handguns with ammunition.

Such was the Gestapo chief's implementation of Nazism's strident "last man, last round" propaganda.

Himmler's flight and capture

Even Heinrich Himmler, Hitler's most dedicated disciple whom der Fuhrer had called "my faithful Heinrich," joined henchmen fleeing southward with as much booty as they could manage.

After an impassioned address to officers of a Grenadier Division, urging them to "seize every man who turns back" and shoot them against a wall, on the 20th May, Himmler put on an eyepatch and the uniform of the Field Security Police, and decamped.

The efficient policeman and evil genius of the German horror camps carried a pass in the name of Heinrich Hitzinger. This false identification was that of a man resembling Himmler, who had been condemned to death by a "People's Court." No doubt it had been culled from the massive files of the Main Security Office.

It was, in fact, this carefully prepared forgery that was eventually Himmler's undoing. Among the millions of refugees and displaced persons crowding the roads of a disintegrating Germany, few had any kind of iron-clad ID documents. When such papers were produced, Allied officers were immediately put on the alert.

That is how it happened in Himmler's case. When he and two aides tried to pass a British check-point, his meticulously correct identity card aroused the suspicions of the military police and he was detained.

A war correspondent, reporting the incident at the time, aptly observed: "He should have known that had he approached that unimportant little bridge at Bremervoerse without papers and pushing a wheel-barrow full of humble possessions, saying he was a refugee making his way home, he would have stood every chance of passing any Allied troops he encountered."[1]

But to Himmler's Gestapo mind, it was unthinkable that he could travel anywhere without an official credential. Under the system established by him, any man without an ID card was a prey for the police.

Himmler was taken to a vacant two-storey villa in Lueneberg to be interrogated by Capt. Tom Silvester. Realizing that the game was over, he removed his eye-patch, put on the familiar steel-rimmed glasses, and in a very quiet voice, said: "Heinrich Himmler."

His British captors then stripped him of all his clothing, which they searched for the poison top Nazis were known to carry when they became fugitives. Medical men made a cursory examination of his mouth, but did not find anything. But when they decided upon a second and more thorough inspection, Himmler snapped shut his jaws and crushed a small phial of poison he carried concealed behind his teeth. He toppled to the floor.

There was no antidote for the poison and efforts to revive the important prisoner were futile.

The following day American troops in Berchtesgaden unearthed Himmler's secret hoard of currency. It amounted to about a million dollars in banknotes of 26 countries, hidden beneath the floor of a barn. Oddly enough, the cache contained no U.S. money.

Very few of the senior SS officers followed Himmler's example and chose suicide as a way out. Some were caught and sentenced to periods of imprisonment, then released. Some followed the prearranged escape route — from Munich into Austria, across the Alps into Italy and, helped by Bishop Hudal at the Vatican, on to South America and freedom.

An unknown number were secretly incorporated into supposedly non-political police troops such as the *Landjaeger* or rural gendarmerie.

A handful simply vanished.

Among the latter was SS General Heinrich Müller, chief of the Gestapo. He is of interest because his former associates believe he went over to the Russians, taking some of the secret police files with him, and may still be alive in the USSR, working for the KGB.

Schellenberg reports that Müller had established contact with the Russian Secret Service in late 1943 and became a Soviet agent.

Like others of the Nazi police establishment, Müller wanted ''to build up a central card index, with an individual card for every living German and, of course, with a precise note on any 'dubious episode,' no matter how trivial."[2]

What Müller did not provide the Russians in dossier form he probably recited from memory. He was widely known among his police colleagues for the amazing amount of material he kept filed in his head. It was said that he could recall at once the name of even some unimportant agent in a small village abroad. "Certainly, no other police expert possesses so wide a knowledge of personalities and at the same time has so deep an insight into political events, a detailed knowledge of which is still important to this very day."[3]

Interpol files recovered

At Interpol's Wansee headquarters, files which had survived the destruction of war and the looting that followed, were recovered in July 1945 by Allied occupation forces active under authority of the Public Safety Officer of Berlin.

Their official report states that these files included the following:

1) A card index consisting of "every subject whose record was referred to IKPK [Interpol] since its inception." However, the register to which the index referred had disappeared.

2) An index of persons about whom Interpol had circularized information.

3) Index cards recording cancellations of some circulations in the preceding file.

4) Index cards relating to counterfeit currencies.

5) A file relating to stolen jewelry and works of art.

6) Index of subjects whose description slips, fingerprints and photographs had been circulated by Himmler's Amt V.

Color tabs were used to designate each subject's country of birth. A former employee of the Nazi Interpol said the file was far from complete. Curiously, about one third of the section classifying pickpockets was missing.

7) A complete envelope file for the period 1929 to 1939 of circular slips, photographs and fingerprints of persons circularized outside regular publication.

8) Two drawers of old indexes brought from Vienna in the 1941 transfer. These did not appear to be usable, owing to the fact that they did not refer to any currently existing records.

The Allied military authorities noted in their memorandum concerning the files that Swiss police officials had already "informally" expressed great interest in having them as a nucleus around which to reconstitute Interpol.

In this connection, it is noteworthy that the last issue of the Interpol magazine, dated 20 February 1945 and published by the Nazis, carried the name of Col. Werner Mueller, Chief of Security Police and Criminal Police in Berne, Switzerland, as a member of the editorial committee.

"Since these files were originally established under legitimately international auspices," wrote the US member of the committee drafting the report, "it would be improper to deal with them as German. They might more properly be turned over to an international organization for police cooperation, when such is created."

The report then went on to make a recommendation in language that could only have come from some official of Interpol itself. It suggested "that the Allied Control Authority hold these files in security until such time as a quasi-public association of police executive officers, with international membership, having as its object international cooperation in combatting crime, shall be formed and shall establish a headquarters office, a division of which shall be devoted to the circularization of international or migratory criminals."

There it was —the blueprint for the reintegration and continuity of Interpol. The proposal was spelled out in the orotund phrases first heard in the assembly halls of the various prewar congresses, later to be embodied in the organization's constitution and in its image-building handouts to the press.

The official memorandum added that once Interpol had regrouped and set up an administrative centre, the Allied Control Authority should "thereupon turn the above-described files over to the headquarters office of the international police executives' association."

The Interpol follow-up

Not long after this report was sent to the Directorate of the Allied Control Authority (I.A. & C. Division), the Police Safety Committee received a letter dated 4 March 1946 from Florent Louwage, Inspector General of Belgian Police and a member of Interpol's executive committee during the time that organization was under Nazi domination.

Inspector Louwage informed the Allied authorities that he had learned that documents belonging to Interpol, which had been transferred from Vienna to Wansee, were now in safekeeping at the military government's Berlin Documents Center. Acting in his capacity as Interpol's permanent reporter, he requested that the files be turned over to him.

In addition to the Interpol archives, he also asked for the organization's funds, which Nazi officials had deposited in the Deutsche Bank in Berlin-Zehlendorf.

The Public Safety Committee located two bank accounts, one with a balance of 13,000 marks and the second 12,000 marks. Trustees of the funds were Oskar Dressler and Dr. Karl Zindel, both deceased.

The Military Government conducted an inquiry into the history and legal aspects of Interpol's cash reserves, as well as their intended use. Persuaded that Louwage's claim was a legitimate one, they ordered that both funds and files be turned over to the committee he had formed for re-establishing the organization.

There is no evidence to suggest that the files taken over from the Nazi archives after five years of use by the minions of such men as Himmler, Heydrich, Kaltenbrunner and Müller, were ever reviewed or purged in any way.

Writing in the April 1950 issue of Interpol's confidential magazine, Paul Marabuto of the General Secretariat in Paris explained the great number of Jewish names in Interpol's archives, not as Nazi hold-overs, but in terms of religious identity. Comparing Jewish criminals with those of the Catholic faith, Marabuto declared:

"Jews hardly ever participate in offences which require a man to drift away from society and to adopt a purely passive attitude. On the other hand, they seem to be more inclined to offences with a materialistic purpose to them. But what, above all, appears from statistical comparison, is the preference which Jewish offenders have for offences which require the use of craftiness and, similarly, their hatred for violence. This statistical fact is in contradiction with assertions of pre-war German propagandists; it explains, on the other hand, why the ICPC [Interpol] which is particularly concerned with eliminating swindling, monetary or otherwise, has so many Jewish names in its files."[4]

This Shylock stereotype of the Jew, seen as the cunning, materialistic swindler — far from being a contradiction of Nazi propaganda — was in fact a restatement of it.

> *"Totalitarianism can be regarded not only as a
> description of developments in Russia and
> Germany in the nineteen-thirties, but as a
> potentiality in any 20th century society."*
> — Richard Reinitz

6. *International Big Brotherhood*

In less than four months after Allied authorities had turned
over to him Interpol's remaining files and bank accounts,
Belgian Police Inspector F. E. Louwage convened a meeting to
initiate a full-scale restoration of the organization.

A committee of five met early in June 1946 at Brussel's Palais
de Justice to lay the groundwork. All were personal friends
and members of the "old boy network" of international
police. They were, besides Louwage: Harry Soderman,
Swedish criminologist; Wernher Müller, chief of Swiss Federal Police; Louis Ducloux, chief of detectives in France's

Sureté Nationale; and Ronald Howe, assistant Commissioner of Scotland Yard.

Of the five conferees, only Howe had not been linked with Interpol during the war years.

Florent Louwage, a career policeman, had served in the Belgian Intelligence Service during the first World War, and as chief of Internal Security under Nazi occupation during the second.

It is not generally known that Belgium was one of thirteen countries which made a secret prewar agreement with Heydrich when the latter decided to set up a kind of second Interpol controlled by the Gestapo. His plan was to use the personal contacts he had made through Interpol with the ranking police authorities throughout Europe to form a political intelligence nexus that would enable the Germans to halt Communist infiltration.

Germany, it will be recalled, did not send a representative to the 1937 Interpol congress in London. Instead, Heydrich secretly invited a select group of delegates to a clandestine meeting held two months later in Berlin.

The thirteen nations that joined the Nazis in this 1937 compact were: Brazil, Poland, Belgium, Holland, Yugoslavia, Greece, Italy, Japan, Bulgaria, Finland, Hungary, Portugal and Spain.

Six of these cooperating powers were later to go to war with Germany; and all but one of these six — Brazil — were overrun and occupied within three years by the German forces.

Allied intelligence learned of the secret prewar agreements after Germany surrendered in 1945. A report with the word "Geheim" (Secret) stamped in red across the top had been overlooked when the Gestapo hastily dismantled their archives, just before the defending forces around Berlin collapsed.

The document was a memorandum which Reinhard Heydrich had sent to Herman Goering. In a covering letter, dated

22 August 1938, Heydrich assured Goering of having had "notable success" with his plan to secure the confidential cooperation of Germany's police friends.

"As far as written agreements were made with foreign police," he wrote, "they correspond with the attached form, No. 2, with insignificant differences.

"Of all the countries named in Enclosure No. 1 — except Rumania — authorized police representatives have been guests of the German police in Germany, in some cases frequently. The meeting of police representatives in Germany in August — September 1937 brought about personal contacts among police leaders, laying a solid foundation for the favourable development of international cooperation of political police . . ."[1]

Post-war revival

Acting upon Inspector Louwage's call for a postwar reconstruction of Interpol, the Belgian government sent out invitations to all former members asking them to come to Brussels for the first conference, scheduled for June 3, 1946.

When the Belgian ambassador in· Washington presented the note soliciting U.S. participation in the Brussels meeting, the official reaction behind the scenes was one of extreme caution. The State Department sent an urgent, confidential message to the U.S. Embassy in Brussels asking for further information:

"We assume this is same organization founded Vienna 1923 taken under Nazi domination 1932 and headquarters moved Berlin at which time U.S. ceased relationship."

The telegram went on to request data concerning the history and background of the Belgian sponsorship; a list of the governments likely to be represented at the assembly; and any indication of what Interpol's future plans were.

Secretary of State James F. Byrnes also asked the Attorney General for his opinion of sending a U.S. delegate to the congress. The latter replied that "it is my studied recommendation that no representative of the Government of the United States be designated to attend this meeting."

The Attorney General pointed out that as a result of the war, the majority of the European police departments had not yet been re-established sufficiently "to permit the undertaking of efficient police programs."

That was a diplomatic way of reminding State that the U.S. was at the moment busy with its own programme of denazifying and decentralizing the territories formerly under the control of Himmler and his terror legions.

He concluded by saying: "In addition, I believe that the criticism arising from the selection of countries will more than offset any possible benefit that would accrue from such a meeting."

After carefully weighing the matter, the State Department sent the Belgian government a polite note asking that the U.S. be excused from attending the Brussels conclave.

But, if both the Secretary of State and the Attorney General properly adopted a wait-and-see attitude toward an Interpol so hastily resurrected from the Nazi ruins, J. Edgar Hoover did not. The Director was ready at once to rejoin his former colleagues. Although nominally under the supervision of the Department of Justice, Hoover acted on his own as was his wont. He independently dispatched Norton R. Telford, FBI representative in Paris, to confer with Louwage and his immediate circle, who were planning the Brussels conference.

Whether Telford, or the top G-man himself, actually attended the meeting as a non-delegate is not known. Interpol's official organ, *International Criminal Police Review*, reported that the representatives of the U.S. and Greece were "absent."

However, recently uncovered documentary evidence strongly suggests that whether or not an FBI agent was present at the proceedings, is an academic question. The fact is that Hoover had already privately established a working liaison with Louwage and his committee. In doing so, he contravened the stated policy and orders of his superiors in the U.S. government.

The true state of affairs emerged the following year when the annual meeting was held in Paris, where the Brussels delegates had voted to establish permanent Interpol headquarters. Invitations were sent through the usual diplomatic channels; but the U.S. Secretary of State soon learned that this customary protocol had been breached. J. Edgar Hoover had pre-empted the option.

Replying to the State Department's customary request for an opinion on the advisability of sending an official delegate to the Paris convention, Attorney General Tom Clark informed Secretary Acheson:

"At the annual meeting of the International Criminal Commission in Brussels, Belgium in 1946, Mr. J. Edgar Hoover, Director of the Federal Bureau of Investigation was elected Vice President. Upon his acceptance of this elective post, steps were taken to make the Federal Bureau of Investigation an official member of the Commission."

Clark further informed the State Department that Hoover had already designated FBI Agent Norton R. Telford a delegate to the Paris conference. "Mr. Telford," he wrote, "has received appropriate instructions from Mr. Hoover to represent that Bureau at the General Assembly."

And that was that. By fiat of the Director, the U.S. was once again a participating member of Interpol.

Hoover remained an enthusiastic supporter of the organization until the Czech refugee incident of 1950, described in previous pages of this work. At that time, he officially withdrew FBI representation, but later, after the Treasury Department was designated the U.S. arm of Interpol, he permitted a link-up between the National Crime Center computer and Interpol's Washington Bureau.

Even after Hoover formally resigned from Interpol in 1950, U.S. participation continued on a non-member basis.

Supplanting the FBI as the U.S. link to Interpol was the Treasury Department. As early as 1948 — two years before Hoover resigned from the association — James J. Maloney, chief of the Secret Service, suggested in a memorandum to administrative assistant William W. Parsons that active participation in Interpol's activities "might be beneficial not only to the Secret Service, but also to other Treasury Department law-enforcement agencies."

"Informal" participation

There is evidence that Treasury representatives attended Interpol conclaves as observers, and cooperated "informally" with the organization until legislation was passed in 1958 legally empowering the Attorney General to designate that Department as the U.S. arm of Interpol.

Myles Ambrose, who formerly coordinated Treasury's enforcement and intelligence activities, bringing closer together the operations of IRS, the Secret Service and Coast Guard, led the official U.S. delegation to the association's annual assemblies until he left Treasury in 1960.

His successor, Eugene Rossides, continued the close cooperation between Treasury agencies and Interpol, which Ambrose had begun. In 1969 he was elected vice-president of the organization, serving with President Paul Dickopf of Germany.

According to Vaughn Young, director of research for the National Commission On Law Enforcement and Social Justice, it was while Rossides was IP vice-president that he received a call from then-Representative Gerald Ford.

"A man from upstate New York by the name of G. Gordon Liddy needed a job. Could Rossides help out? Rossides did, and Liddy, a former CIA agent destined to become the most colorful of the Watergate conspirators was posted as a Treasury Special Assistant and given an office 'a few doors down the hall' from Interpol."

Young adds that "apparently, Liddy fit the Interpol in-crowd. U.S. Bureau of Customs Chief Myles Ambrose, also an Interpol delegate, was reported escorting Liddy around one of his Washington parties, introducing him to guests."[3]

After Rossides' resignation from Treasury was announced on December 5, 1972, he was replaced by Edward L. Morgan, who the following year headed the U.S. delegation to Interpol's annual congress, meeting in Vienna. At that assembly he was elected a member of the IP Executive Committee.

This nine-man panel is composed of Interpol's president (elected by the General Assembly to a four-year term); two vice-presidents and six delegates from different member countries. To maintain the organization's international character, the constitution requires that the president and vice-presidents shall be from different continents. Likewise, in selecting the delegates on the Executive Committee, consideration is given to providing as wide a geographical representation as possible.

While the General Assembly is nominally the body of supreme authority, Interpol is, for all practical purposes, controlled by the permanent General Secretary who is French.

This fact became evident in May 1975, when Secretary General Jean Nepote refused to honor the request of Interpol Washington for a list of Interpol employees, officers and staff members, together with a brief description of their professional background.

This information, as M. Nepote was aware, had been solicited by a U.S. Senate Committee then holding hearings to learn more about the structure and operation of a global police agency which has access to sensitive data concerning individual U.S. citizens. But his refusal was in accord with Article 30 of the Interpol constitution, which states: "In the exercise of their duties, the Secretary General and the staff shall neither solicit nor accept instructions from any government or authority outside the Organization."

The inability of the Washington NCB to obtain the required facts concerning the Paris personnel provided a patent illustration of the organization's independent status.

The Watergate explosion cut short Edward Morgan's term as an Interpol executive. He resigned after investigators looking into President Nixon's financial affairs learned that Morgan had illegally backdated a document reporting the Chief Executive's donation of private papers to the National Archives, thus providing a $576,000 income-tax deduction. At the time of this resignation, Morgan told an interviewer: "The tanks are coming. They're coming right down Pennsylvania Avenue and into the Oval Office."

Morgan later pleaded guilty and was sentenced to four months in jail and 20 months probation.

Oddly enough, Morgan's position as an executive of Interpol went virtually unnoticed in the profusion of news stories which appeared reporting his "one terrible mistake in an effort to serve with misplaced loyalty."

Watergate was the big story, of course; and it was perhaps only natural that the press would overlook what might appear just an added detail.

At the same time, it preserved intact Interpol's long record of being able to remain in a snug harbor when violent political gales were blowing.

> *"When an agency of the U.S. Government is authorized to transmit information about its citizens to a foreign government, uneasiness is even more pronounced."*
>
> — Sen. Joseph Montoya

7. *Keeping Tabs on the World*

It is quite remarkable that a global organization having close ties to the world's major police systems could exist half a century without coming under the close scrutiny of any government.

But Interpol did precisely that.

While it is true that a special subcommittee of the U.S. Congress in 1959 made a report on the history and activities of Interpol, the review fell far short of being either completely accurate or a study in depth. It was based, in fact, upon conversations which committee members had with police officials in several European cities and with the Secretary General of Interpol — all of them strong advocates of the organization.

Indeed, much of the language used in the report to define Interpol's objectives and describe its function was lifted verbatim from the association's own literature.

A naiveté, which so often afflicts U.S. Congressmen on foreign fact-finding missions, shows itself plainly in several of the conclusions stated in the paper. For example, it is affirmed that one of the chief concerns of the subcommittee was whether Interpol was susceptible of being used in any way by other countries for political activities. After discussing this question with the organization's General Secretary in Paris, the honorable members reached the firm opinion that there is no need for concern. Their reason: such a misuse of Interpol intelligence is contrary to that body's constitution! This is the same as asserting that because the U.S. Constitution guarantees that Americans shall be secure in their homes and papers against unreasonable government intrusion, law-enforcement agents do not engage in illegal trespass, wiretapping, bugging, interception of mail, and compiling of secret dossiers. The truth is that they do all these things on a growing and massive scale, with impunity and in flagrant violation of the law.

The 1959 report notes that during the Congressmen's conversations with Interpol's Secretary General in Paris, the hope was expressed that the Federal Bureau of Investigation might consider renewing its participation in Interpol. The rationale for such an aspiration was candidly stated:

"Interpol is interested in the FBI's participation because of its tremendous files from which, upon proper request, information could be made available to Interpol."

As we have previously seen, FBI Director J. Edgar Hoover refused to rejoin Interpol; but did place at the disposal of 122 foreign countries his agency's "tremendous files," for which they so fervently yearned.

One accurate statistic cited in the report is of considerable interest because of its comparison value. It records that "the authorized appropriation for U.S. membership may not exceed $25,000 yearly. Present dues of the United States is $11,000 yearly."

According to figures provided Congress by Interpol Washington, the U.S. dues in 1975 were $140,000. In addition, during 1974-1975, the Treasury Department made "a one-time, non-recurring voluntary contribution of $135,000." This sum was not reflected in the summary of estimated costs to be incurred by the U. S. Government with regard to the operation of Interpol during the fiscal year 1975. That total came to $528,492.

Curiously enough, the $135,000 donation was not made directly to Interpol by the Treasury Department, which has official liaison with that organizaton, but by the Agency For International Development (AID). Sheldon Vance of the U.S. State Department who approved the reallocation of the funds later admitted to an interviewer that he found the procedure "odd."[1]

A spokesman for Interpol's NCB in Washington said the funds came from the Foreign Assistance Funds For International Narcotics Control and were intended to support an Interpol liaison officer in both Southeast Asia and Latin America during 1975 and 1976.

Neither of these officers is American. The Federal Drug Enforcement Agency has two of its officers assigned to Interpol, but their salaries and expenses are paid from that agency's regular budget. (The agent currently posted to Interpol Paris has a civil service grade-step rating of GS12, which calls for an annual salary of $18,463.)

It is especially ironical that part of the $135,000 U.S. contribution was to be spent on Interpol's operations in Latin America. A secret report made available to me by a Mexican official of credibility and standing reveals that some of the major traffickers in three South American countries are present or former Interpol agents.

The memorandum contains the names of no fewer than 14 Interpol agents either currently or formerly involved in an important cocaine trafficking network which employs courier routes to Brazil, Paraguay, Argentina and the U.S.

Members of the network have been practically immune from prosecution because they enjoyed the protection of the Interpol chief in their country. When couriers have been apprehended carrying the drug, they have been released after the Interpol bureau chief identified them as his agents.

One former Interpol chief kept one half of all the cocaine confiscated by his officers and sold it to intermediaries who returned it to the traffic.

Extortion is also a common practice among the crooked Interpol officials. In 1973, in a typical instance, one group of U.S. traffickers arrested in a South American country paid the Interpol bureau chief $40,000 to obtain their release.

Numerous other cases of extortion, bribery and protection payoffs have occurred and are still occurring in South America, all of them involving Interpol agents.

I have examined documents which indicate that these activities have been known to top-level officials at Interpol headquarters for some time. But, just as the FBI would not prosecute its own delinquent agents, because it would reflect unfavorably on the Bureau, so Interpol has concealed the criminal conduct of IP officers.

The Montoya hearing

Sen. Joseph Montoya, who had earlier expressed his concern about the potential threat to civil liberties inherent in Interpol's international network, explored the problem at closer range. On May 6, 1975, he summoned Treasury's assistant secretary for enforcement operations before his Subcommittee on Appropriations for a hearing on the subject.

The Treasury official — David R. Macdonald — was accompanied by his deputy, James B. Clawson; and by Louis B. Sims, chief of Interpol's National Central Bureau.

While the answers to Sen. Montoya's questions were sometimes unforthcoming and at other times misleading or factually incorrect, the session did throw a great deal of light into some heretofore murky corners of Interpol's secret world.

Testimony revealed, for example, that Interpol has access not only to FBI's National Crime Information Center, but also to another information warehouse maintained by the Government, known as TECS.

TECS, it appears, is the acronym for Treasury Enforcement Communications System. A terminal of this computer complex is located in Interpol's Washington office.

According to chief Louis B. Sims, TECS contains information "of a criminal enforcement nature," inserted into it by the U.S. Customs Service; the Bureau of Alcohol, Tobacco and Firearms; the IRS; and by Interpol itself.

Sen. Montoya produced a fact sheet on TECS which disclosed publicly for the first time that the system has telecommunication terminals located in Treasury law-enforcement facilities throughout the United States; and is connected to a master Computer Center in San Diego, California.

Moreover, it has on-line access to the FBI National Crime Computer in Washington; and an interface with the National Law Enforcement Telecommunications System (NLETS) which provides message-switching capability with enforcement agencies in all 50 States.

The records to which these terminals have immediate access include not only individuals with prior criminal histories, but persons " of current investigative interest," which might conceivably be anyone in the U.S.

Replying to Sen. Montoya's question as to whether the only input from IRS Intelligence Division was information concerning persons for whom an arrest warrant was outstanding, Chief Sims said:

"It is my understanding that they do put selective criminal type investigations in there, where the individual perhaps isn't the subject of an arrest warrant yet, but they are seeking that individual for the purpose of investigation."

Further questioning elicited the admission that Interpol has been used by IRS to locate U.S. citizens in foreign countries. As tax violations are not extraditable crimes in other countries, such action by Interpol was in direct violation of its own regulations. It also contradicted an earlier prepared statement made to the Committee by Assistant Secretary Macdonald. He asserted that an investigative request sent to any Interpol member country "must be in accord with the laws of the country receiving the request, as well as being related to a criminal offense *in both countries*." (Emphasis added.) The U.S. is virtually unique among the 122 member States of Interpol in regarding tax evasion as a major crime. Switzerland has had to officially remind the U.S. of this fact when demands have been made for bank records. Moreover, when an IRS secret agent was discovered spying on American tourists at a Swiss ski resort, he was expelled from the country.

The question of Interpol's access to the FBI's vast, computerized NCIC files came up in the course of the hearing and the customary reassurances concerning its confidentiality repeated. Sen. Montoya had inserted into the record a letter he had received from FBI Director Clarence Kelley, in which Kelley made once again the oft-heard observation that Interpol does not have *direct* access to the National Crime Information Center data bank. He added that "the information in the NCIC is only available indirectly to Interpol through the National Central Bureau and TECS linkage to the NCIC."[2]

Apparently we are meant to accept this assertion in the same spirit that we would if informed that the FBI archives are under the personal supervision of the Recording Angel.

Instead, one recalls the cautionary words a short time previously of Kelley's boss, President Gerald Ford. In a speech before a college audience Ford declared:

"Leaving the protection of individual privacy to government officials has been compared to asking the fox to protect the chicken coop."

In a strictly technical sense, in any case, Interpol does have direct access to the NCIC, since the chief of Interpol Washington is a de facto employee of the police organization.

The ambiguity of a private, foreign organization being housed, staffed and financed as an official arm of the federal government has yet to be legally resolved.

Quite aside from the problem of NCIC, it was disclosed during Chief Sim's testimony before the committee that the computer bank is not Interpol's only source of data from FBI files.

Asked by Sen. Montoya if the U.S. office of Interpol obtains information from the FBI by other means than the NCIC, Chief Sims replied, "Yes, sir, on occasion we do." He went on to admit that an agent from Interpol goes in person to the FBI headquarters liaison office, where he is given information from the Bureau's intelligence files.

Director Kelley said in his letter to the Montoya committee that the basic authority for the NCIC program is derived from Title 38, U.S. Code, Section 534, which authorizes the Attorney General "to acquire, collect, classify and preserve identification, criminal identification, crime and other records and exchange these records with and for the official use of authorized officials of the Federal Government, the states, cities, penal and other institutions." The Attorney General in turn, says Kelley, delegated that authority to the Director of the FBI.

Even if one accepts the sweeping — and it may well be, unconstitutional — powers spelled out in the foregoing spate of legalese, it is difficult if not impossible to find in it any specific authority for linking the NCIC to Interpol or for passing on to its representatives information from the FBI files.

As in the case of the majority of government files, in all probability no statutory authority exists. The global expansion of the dossier system has been by administrative ukase, not by legislative enactment.

Top-Secret clearance

Not even top-security documents need be withheld from the American arm of Interpol because of being classified material. In response to the question: What level of Security clearance is held by Interpol members in the U.S.?, Louis Sims testified that not only Interpol executives, but the entire clerical and administrative staff are cleared for *Top Secret*.[3]

Information provided the Senate committee by the NCB in Washington revealed that there are 10 full-time employees on the U.S. staff, one of which is assigned to the Paris headquarters. The remaining nine occupy, rent-free, six offices and one reception area in the Treasury Department Building in the Nation's Capital.

In addition to the regular Treasury Department personnel assigned to Interpol, but paid by the U.S. government, two agents from the Drug Enforcement Agency also work with the organization, one in Washington and one in Paris. (The American Embassy in Paris is a receiving point for all telex messages from the U.S. to Interpol.)

In the course of his questioning, Sen. Montoya pinpointed one of the principal threats to civil liberties posed by the export to foreign countries of information on private citizens.

While allegedly sought for legitimate law-enforcement purposes, could it not, if fact, be used for quite different ends?

Such a concern is seen to be justified when it is recalled that of Interpol's 122 members only a minority are democracies holding the same view of due process as that prevailing in, say, Britain or the U.S.A.

Interpol's response to the issue cannot be considered very satisfactory, as shown by the following exchange on the subject.

Sen. MONTOYA. Have those charges from abroad turned out to be well-founded and were they carried through?

Mr. SIMS. Yes, sir, I make a habit also, whenever a request is initiated in the investigative stage, of asking them if they would follow up on it, provide us with the conclusion of the investigation and in the event of arrest to provide fingerprints.

Sen. MONTOYA. What is your batting average?

Mr. SIMS. Pretty good. I would say that probably 8 out of 10 come back with information, even if I didn't ask for it.

Sen. MONTOYA. No, I am referring to the fact that a foreign police department wanted information on a certain individual and they state as a premise that he was charged with a crime or is being investigated for a crime. Do you have any way of ascertaining in how many instances that individual was successfully prosecuted?

Mr. SIMS. I don't have any way of ascertaining that other than just knowing that I see every case that goes out — at some stage.

Sen. MONTOYA. You only see the case when it comes in and prior to prosecution?

Mr. MACDONALD. He means long after the information has been provided.

Mr. SIMS. When a case is at the investigative stage, we consider it to be an open case. We have a suspense system. That is one of the reasons we have received the answer that we have asked for. If we haven't received it, we sent back another letter or message.

Sen. MONTOYA. Do you require that the Interpol office in the foreign country to notify you as to what happens to that particular individual about whom you supplied information?

Mr. SIMS. Yes, sir. We ask for that.

Sen. MONTOYA. Do you keep a record here of what happens to those individuals?

Mr. SIMS. We do; but it is in each individual case file.

Sen. MONTOYA. Can you give me the statistics as to how many of the individuals on which information was supplied were successfully prosecuted?

Mr. SIMS. I have no statistics on this.
Sen. MONTOYA. Then you don't get that information?

Mr. SIMS. Yes, sir, but it is included in the individual file and there are no statistics compiled for that purpose.

Sen. MONTOYA. Why don't you? Is it not a matter of great concern whether the foreign governments are really legitimately asking for information or whether they are trying to play games with you in the name of law enforcement?

Mr. SIMS. I agree with your concept completely. However, the only way the information is handled is on an individual basis. It is kept in a pending status until we are satisfied with the information. If I don't get it, I ask for it. That is the reason I do not have over-all statistics. [Sic.]

Sen. MONTOYA. It is very strange that you do get requests for information from foreign countries about American citizens and you are not keeping a statistical record on whether or not the information was actually utilized toward the final objective of pressing charges against that individual in a foreign country."[4]

A permanent record

The Interpol representative admitted under questioning that the Paris headquarters of the organization maintains numerous files containing information on U.S. citizens, supplied both by the Washington NCB and by other countries. Sen. Montoya then asked whether any attempt is made to purge these files, or whether, once information has been entered in the dossiers, it is retained as a permanent record.

Louis Sims replied, "I think it remains as a permanent record."

Sims asserted that the U.S. Central Bureau would not transmit data dealing with the personal habits of individuals, "unless they concern criminal activities." In practice, such a loophole is large indeed, since "criminal activities" is an inexact term which often includes activities for which an individual or a group would not and could not be prosecuted in their own country, but would be considered a serious offense in certain other countries.

Moreover, Sims acknowledged the possibility that foreign police may send personal information on American citizens to the General Secretary in Paris, to be filed and re-transmitted throughout the world. Neither Interpol U.S. nor any agency of the government has effective control over these transmissions. (As we shall later show, in fact, certain federal agencies are themselves the most prolific sources of such information, which is made available to foreign officials.)

Even worse, it has been reported that U.S. citizens abroad especially those who are suspected of drug offences, have been "fingered" by American agents, who have urged foreign police to deal harshly with them.

A typical case is that of an American couple, Mr. and Mrs. James Philip Morton. According to an Associated Press account, Morton and his wife were beaten and tortured for five hours at the Mexico City airport, the police ripping off the wife's earrings from her pierced ears, tearing the lobes.

"For five hours," declared Morton, "we were both exposed to violent fist and club beatings, electric shock by cattle prods even."

Philip Millard, of Alameda, California, another U.S. citizen imprisoned in Mexico affirmed:

"Lawyers tell us that the U.S. Government is pressing the Mexican Government to go as hard on us as it can to make examples of us — a warning to others not to bring drugs through Mexico." He added that he and sixty-seven other inmates of Lecumberri prison were going on a hunger strike "because the U.S. Embassy is subverting justice."

Millard's mother told newsmen that a Mexican lawyer telephoned her soon after her son was arrested and assured her that for $4,000 he could get him out of jail. People of modest means, the Millards took the amount from their retirement money and sent it to the Mexican lawyer. They heard nothing further from him, and another, reputable, legal counsel informed her that the man had done nothing for Philip.

Mrs. Millard said she had talked by telephone with a U.S. official named Donald Tremblay at the U.S. Embassy in Mexico City, who informed her that her son had promised to pay some money to the guards at the prison. "He told us in a delicate way that the money was to assure that our son wouldn't be beaten."

Another of the Millard's sons went in person to Mexico and after talking to Tremblay at the Embassy, delivered $1,000 to the captain of the guards.

When Associated Press queried the U.S. Embassy concerning the incident, officials there refused to comment other than to acknowledge that a Donald Tremblay had formerly worked at the Embassy.[5]

It is important to bear in mind that, while extortion and confidence games are international crimes which Interpol has so often publicly vowed to combat, there is no evidence that any law-enforcement action was taken in the case just recited. On the contrary, the governments of Mexico and the United States, both Interpol members, drew a protective curtain of silence around the whole outrageous affair.

Canadian prisoners in a Mexico City jail also reported that police beat, tortured and tricked them into signing confessions. They complained that they were being treated "as if they were Americans."

Another instance in which agents of the U.S. federal government cooperated with — if, indeed, they did not initiate — the maltreatment of five American and two British nationals, occurred in Madrid, Spain.

Let it be noted at once that all eight of the young people involved in the present case were, without exception, innocent of any law violation. None had a criminal record. All were found to be guiltless at the end of their ordeal.

On 18 November 1972, the Special Narcotics Brigade of the Spanish police arrested the youths in Madrid "on suspicion of trafficking in LSD." For the next two days they were held in custody and interrogated in what they afterward described as "a brutal manner."

One of the suspects declared in a sworn statement that during the time they were being grilled by the police, he was punched and slammed against the wall. He was certain that one of the plainclothes men present at the inquisition was American.

During the time the accused were being held in jail, the Madrid office of the U.S. Bureau of Narcotics and Dangerous Drugs (now the DEA) sent a confidential telex message to that agency's regional offices in Washington, Los Angeles, London and Panama, requesting them to conduct a background investigation on the prisoners. All replied, after a check of their files that the suspects had no criminal record.

The youths were released from custody after the forensic laboratory in Madrid sent the Spanish police a report stating that there was no trace of LSD nor any other narcotic in the chocolate candy they had seized from the group.

In a memorandum to BNDD headquarters in Washington, Special Agent Weldon C. Curry admitted that agents from the bureau's Madrid office had worked with the Spanish police, but explained this action by asserting that "the Spanish DGS requested the assistance of the Madrid D.O. due to the extremely large amount of correspondence written in English, which was involved in this investigation."

Such a statement ignores the fact that the Spanish police have available to them the services of excellent professional translators.

In an "off-the-record" conversation with the writer, a Spanish police official two years later said that a U.S. agent had been present during the interrogation of the suspects. Moreover, he intimated that the arrests had taken place after the Spansh police were "tipped" by a representative of the U.S. Customs office in Madrid.

It is not without significance that all the youths who were involved in the Madrid incident were members of the Church of Scientology. As previously noted, this was one of the religious groups found to be on the Nixon hate list. For years its members have been subjected to surveillance and covert harrassment by federal agents at home and in various countries around the world.

The kind of police intelligence which civil libertarians find so disturbing was precisely that included in the message which Regional Director John L. Kelley, Jr., of the BNND transmitted by telex to Madrid and to Interpol Paris, where it was calculated to plant deep suspicion in the minds of foreign police regarding U.S. citizens.

Although he had been informed that the suspects had no criminal record, Kelley still thought the following statement relevant and necessary to the case:

"The Los Angeles Police Department, bunco division,

states that the Church of Scientology is a haven for 'kooks' and that it's members are drug-oriented."[6]

Aside from being false (Scientologists eschew the taking of dangerous drugs of any kind except as prescribed by a physician) this communication could not by any stretch of the imagination be classified as a "criminal history." It is, rather, a broad, unsupported and untrue indictment of a church membership which numbers in the millions.

It is unsettling to reflect that police files in the U.S. on all levels of government from the FBI down, are filled with defamation of this kind, and that they have now become global lending libraries.

In the case of Interpol, not only law-enforcement agencies, but private individuals and groups are, on occasion, given access to these contaminated dossiers.

Chief Sims answered in the affirmative when asked whether Interpol ever sent information to, or processed information from, a private person.

Information supplied to the Montoya Committee shows that in 1974, for example, Interpol responded to 500 "investigative requests" from Congressmen, private citizens, financial institutions, commercial firms and others, unnamed.

In effect, this meant that the National Central Bureau in Washington had shrugged off a "Privacy of Information" resolution passed by the Interpol general assembly the same year. It urges that in exchanging information the ICPO-Interpol NCBc and the general secretariat take into account the privacy of the individual and *strictly confine the availability of the information to official law-enforcement and criminal justice agencies.*" (Emphasis added.)

A noteworthy fact that emerges from this resolution is that the Interpol General Assembly — supreme authority in the organization — can only urge, it cannot require, member countries to conform to regulations established by the ruling body. The Interpol constitution contains no specific provision for disciplining associates who do not comform to the rules.

No ready answers

Several issues raised by the Senate subcommittee found Interpol's U.S. representatives without ready answers.

Accordingly, Louis Sims, chief of the IP Washington bureau, sent a coded radio-message to the General Secretary in Paris, requesting additional information.

Among the more important questions and replies were the following:

1. *What security checks or clearances are personnel at the General Secretariat required to have; who conducts the investigation and who is responsible for reviewing the investigation to determine if the person is suitable?*

Jean Nepote, the General Secretary replied that "most of the General Secretariat staff members are police officers on active duty or recently retired from active duty; no security checks or clearances are required for them. The non-police personnel recruited and employed by the General Secretariat are residents of France, and we check with the French police to determine whether or not these persons have any criminal records."

M. Nepote said he had the ultimate decision on the hiring of employees.

2. *Have there been any persons employed at the General Secretariat as intelligence agents from their country, and how is this guarded against?*

That problem, replied the General Secretary, had never been encountered. Apparently a non-reader of spy stories, Nepote asserted: "We have never had any reason whatsoever even to suspect any employee of being an intelligence agent." Then, as a clencher, he added that every non-police employee is required to sign a declaration that he (or she) will maintain professional secrecy concerning all matters that come to his knowledge in his daily work.

That was the extent of IP's security measures.

3. *Is there a record and file purging plan or system at the General Secretariat, and if so, what is the schedule for purging files?*

In answer to this query, Paris provided the "guidelines" followed in purging records and files in Interpol's archives.

According to this system, files on persons implicated in what the Secretary General designated "major cases" are never purged. Twenty years after the date on which the last items are entered in the files, the dossiers are transferred to microfilm for easy storage, and the paper files destroyed.

When the subject of a record or dossier is known to have died, his file is destroyed.

Files on persons involved in "minor cases" are destroyed ten years after the date on which the last items are entered in the record.

It must not elude our attention here that even these standards — which many would consider unacceptable — are guidelines, not hard and fast rules that are applied *de rigueur*. The final decision on whether a file is purged or destroyed is made arbitrarily by the Secretary General.

As for dossiers on "minor cases," they can be maintained *ad infinitum,* simply by adding an item of information once every ten years.

It was no doubt the absence of adequate safeguards in Interpol's whole system of data collection and record keeping that Sen. Montoya had in mind when, at the close of the May 6 hearing, he declared:

"I am just trying to alert you to the concern that we have here about the loopholes that exist for gathering information on individuals. If you say you are not doing it in this country, that is not to say that other countries are not transmitting personal information on American citizens.

"I think we ought to be concerned, since we are members of

A section of the extensive dossier files kept at Interpol's headquarters in St. Cloud, near Paris.

Interpol, that Americans should not be victimized or their rights invaded under the Interpol umbrella."

Sen. Montoya indicated a justifiable skepticism when he preceded with a large "if" his citation of the Washington bureau's claim that their personnel were "not doing it in this country."

The immense network of integrated data banks controlled by law-enforcement agencies in America has constituted a prime source of information for Interpol since that organization was resurrected from the cemetery of the Third Reich.

In the ensuing chapters of this book we will examine the main U.S. agencies which provide these many feeder lines to the Paris repository.

> *"Buried in rows upon rows of jealously guarded steel filing cabinets, these dossiers rest like little guided missiles, each with its designated target, waiting to be launched toward the destruction of a reputation and a human life."*

> — Alan Barth

8. *The Hoover Legacy*

When Interpol officials candidly admitted in 1959 that they desired FBI participation because of the Bureau's "tremendous files," they knew full well the magnitude of the archives they coveted.

At no time in human history has there existed a collection of biographical records to compare with them. Yet, the vast accumulation of fingerprints, criminal histories and personal dossiers is still growing. It will occupy an important area of the mammoth new FBI building in Washington — the largest and most costly government edifice ever erected in the nation's capital.

The structure might well be called the Hoover Monument, dedicated as it is to the world's most famous chief of secret police. It is a fitting symbol of the late Director's remarkable ability to create and to rule autocratically for almost half a century the free world's most powerful police agency.

Central to that organization are those ever-expanding confidential records — the life work of J. Edgar Hoover. For, like all secret agents, he was a dedicated file-keeper.

In his voracious drive to add as many specimens as possible to his unique fingerprint collection (200,000,000 of them), Hoover even mounted a public campaign urging all citizens to voluntarily supply their prints for his files. The impression conveyed was that giving prints to the police files was a civic duty, like donating blood to the Red Cross.

Until the practice was halted in late 1975, millions of California motorists who applied for a driver's license were asked to submit to thumbprinting for the document. It was perfectly legal to refuse, but thousands who exercised that right had their names passed secretly to the FBI as print resisters.

When Elmer A. Brown took over as head of the California Department of Motor Vehicles, he said he could find no basis in law for the procedure, and canceled the "service."

"I suppose," he said, "that the theory was that refusing a thumbprint obviously meant that you had something to hide."[1]

Hoover also eagerly acquired data not only from law-enforcement reports and court records, but from every other source he could think of. These included federal regulatory agencies, banks, insurance companies, the Medical Information Bureau, civil service, defense contractors, credit companies, the armed forces, and others.

"He had a file on everybody!" exclaimed President Nixon on one of his famous tapes.[2]

Therein lay Hoover's power, or at least a major portion of it.

"That fellow was a master blackmailer," said William Sullivan, who until 1971 was FBI assistant director, "and he did it with considerable finesse . . ."

More and more instances have recently come to light which corroborate Sullivan's statement. Hoover consistently used secret information dredged up by his agents to bring members of Congress and other important figures into what one FBI source called "our stable."

Influential persons would be discreetly made aware the FBI agents had come across derogatory material about them in the course of other investigations.

"He always did that sort of thing," Hoover's former assistant went on. "The moment he would get something on a senator, he'd send one of the errand boys up and advise the senator that 'We're in the course of an investigation and we, by chance, happened to come up with this data on your daughter. But we wanted you to know this — we realize you'd want to know it. But don't have any concern, no one will ever learn about it.'

"Well, what does that tell the senator? From that time on, the senator's right in his pocket."[3]

When the Director discovered that one congressman was a homosexual, he visited him in person to assure him that this intelligence would be scrupulously guarded against any leak to the public.

Sensitive material of this kind was put into folders marked "Do not file," and were kept in Hoover's private office. (Readers will recall that Heydrich, chief of the Nazi secret police, kept in his office a similar file, labeled *Geheime Reichssache – State Secret.*)

Testifying before a subcommittee of the House Judiciary Committee, U.S. Attorney General Edward Levi said that 164 files marked *O.C.* for "Official and Confidential" were taken from Hoover's inner sanctum to the office of assistant director

W. Mark Felt after the Director's death on May 2, 1972. Some of them, he admitted, contained derogatory information on Presidents, members of Congress, "and others."

Levi reported that these files were later recovered by the Department of Justice. But at the same hearing, Clarence M. Kelley, current FBI director, disclosed under questioning that the OC files had not been the only documents whisked from Hoover's office after his demise.

There were others, Kelley affirmed, that had been removed and taken out to Hoover's home in Washington's exclusive Rock Creek Park.

A former top-ranking FBI official recalled that upon being notified of Hoover's death, his long-time close associate, Clyde Tolson, telephoned then-Attorney General Richard D. Kleindienst and asked him to order the Director's office sealed off.

Kleindienst complied with the request; and acting FBI Director L. Patrick Gray gave Hoover's aides a week to clear out his personal effects.

Tolson moved into his late chief's home. There, together with Helen W. Gandy, Hoover's personal secretary for many years, and J. P. Mohr, another veteran FBI official, he spent weeks going through the material that had been transferred from Hoover's private office.

As executor of Hoover's estate, Tolson had legal control of all the Director's "personal" possessions. However, according to another G-man, it was Mohr who, as he put it, "engineered" the removal of the secret files from FBI headquarters. He described some of the papers as "supersensitive," and said that "Hoover amassed many, many documents — they ran into the thousands. Don't call them files, because they were documents, put in these special containers."

When Tolson died in April 1975, his will designated Mohr as executor of his estate. A short time later, Mohr retired from the FBI. When questioned by officials from the U.S. Department of Justice, who are trying to trace the missing dossiers, Mohr denied any knowledge of their present whereabouts, asserting that he knew of no documents being removed to Hoover's home upon his death, nor from the house when Tolson died.[4]

Political manipulations

During J. Edgar Hoover's long reign, he did not hesitate to use sensitive material from his confidential files for purely political ends. The extent of such machinations is still not known, but enough instances have been unsealed to provide a fair sampling of the operation.

In election campaigns involving candidates who were, on the one hand considered critics of the Bureau or on the other, whose influence in office would be useful to the FBI, Hoover on more than one occasion is reported to have dipped into those secret "containers" in his private office for tactical material.

For example, according to accounts by those closest to the action, Hoover tried to insure the re-election of Rep. J. J. Rooney and other Congressional supporters on the House Appropriation Subcommittee that largely controls the FBI budget, by supplying them with politically damaging "background" information regarding their opponents.[5]

Another case involved Sen. Thomas Eagleton who, in the 1972 Presidential race, was chosen by the Democrats as a running mate for George McGovern. Soon after Eagleton's nomination, information was leaked to the press that in 1960, 1964 and 1966 he had been treated by a psychiatrist with electric shock therapy. When this private medical history was made public, McGovern reluctantly had to ask him to withdraw from the campaign. The disclosure not only seriously damaged Sen. Eagleton's political career, but it likewise adversely affected the Democratic party in a national election.

Later, the *Washington Post* reported that John Erlichman, Watergate conspirator and President Nixon's aide, had passed them surreptitiously to a newsman after receiving them from FBI files.

The gradual deterioriation of the Bureau, which culminated in the disgraceful revelations following J. Edgar Hoover's death ("He had been leaking stuff all over the place": Sullivan), began much earlier than is generally recognized. Previous improprieties (if that is not too mild a word) remained hidden or were quickly painted over by such massive PR efforts as force-fed newstories of gang-busting, laudatory books, motion pictures and a top-rated TV series.

The unpleasant fact is that Hoover was responding to requests from the White House for sensitive information on political opponents as far back as the administration of Franklin Delano Roosevelt. Sometimes the Director didn't wait to be asked, but volunteered the data if he felt that to do so was in his private interest; or when he just wanted to pass on a piquant morsel to titillate the man in the Oval Office.

With successive Presidents, the evil practice grew. It eventually involved wiretaps on all key government officials, a number of newsmen, and political foes.

The worst Presidential offenders according to William Sullivan whose memorandum was based on 30 years service in the FBI, were Franklin Delano Roosevelt and Lyndon B. Johnson.

On a number of occasions, F.D.R. asked the FBI to spy upon the private lives of his enemies and to call off investigations of political allies and friends. Although he went on record before a Senate committee as vehemently opposed to wiretapping, which he called "an instrument for the oppression of free citizens," Roosevelt nevertheless had Hoover wiretap several Presidential aides. He also called for a name check of citizens who were opposing U.S. entry into the war in 1940.

When Sumner Welles, Undersecretary of State in the Roosevelt cabinet, was being investigated by police for suspected homosexual offenses, F.D.R. had the FBI intervene to halt the inquiry.

Even Eleanor Roosevelt, the President's wife, made "some unusual requests" of the Bureau, nature and number undisclosed.

Lyndon Johnson, who often declared that "F.D.R. was like a daddy to me," followed in his mentor's footsteps but went much further.

In an anonymous letter sent by FBI agents in Los Angeles to then-Attorney General Ramsey Clark, it was reported that "Hoover has stated that the President's first request after taking over the White House was for about 1200 dossiers from confidential files on Johnson's political adversaries, and the number has increased since that time. I am sure you know that this is blackmail."[8]

Hoover, who knew that Johnson "had a voracious appetite for gossip," regularly supplied him with details of the sexual capers of leading personalities. "He listened to the tapes that even had the noises of bedsprings," Time magazine reported, and slapped his thighs with delight when the FBI sent him a report about a prominent Republican senator who patronized a fashionable brothel in Chicago "and had some kinky sexual preferences, all of which were reported in detail." The magazine added that the information came from a madam who was an FBI informer.[9]

This lady of the house was not the only one of her profession to have stoked the files of Hoover's private archives. Following the example set by Gestapo Chief Reinhard Heydrich with his Kitty Salon, the FBI bugged two Washington bordellos in the mid-1960s, hoping to catch foreign diplomats in "compromising situations." Instead, the hidden microphones picked up and recorded on tape the amorous escapades of congressmen, top-ranking bureaucrats and other prominent Americans. J. Edgar Hoover obligingly sent the information collected from these sources to the late President from Pedernales.[10]

While Johnson apparently enjoyed sharing with Hoover the pornography yielded by Director's electronic traps, he was outraged at the slightest indication that he or members of his staff might be the victims of "dirty tricks" perpetrated by his enemies.

Thus when, on the eve of the 1964 election, Johnson's chief aide, Walter Jenkins, was arrested on a homosexual charge, the President asked the FBI to investigate the incident with a view to uncovering a possible connection between the man caught with Jenkins in the YMCA and two members of the Republican National Committee.

When he learned that Jenkins had not been framed, Johnson asked the Bureau to establish a link between Jenkins and Republican Presidential candidate Barry Goldwater. He said Goldwater would find it difficult to deny that he knew Jenkins well personally."

As a final strategem, Johnson asked the agency to persuade Jenkins' doctor to issue a statement saying that his patient was suffering from a brain disease. After examining Jenkins, the doctor refused.

That Hoover was sympathetic to Jenkins' plight was evident in the fact that he reportedly criticized the Washington Police Department for arresting the President's executive assistant. Hoover sent a bouquet of roses to Jenkins at the hospital where the disgraced aide had taken refuge from effects of the scandal, and assigned a top aide to assist Jenkins during his interrogation by other FBI agents.

There is little doubt that Hoover had long maintained a confidential file on Jenkins, as he did on all Government employees in important positions.

But while he displayed what *Time* described as an "almost obsessive condemnation of illicit sexual activities of public figures," like all secret-file keepers, he appears to have applied a friend-or-foe double standard to his dossiers when leaking their contents to incumbent Presidents or to the media.

In Lyndon Johnson, Hoover found a President who saw eye to eye with the FBI's aims and methods, and who was quick to put them to good use in his own service. During the Democratic national convention in 1964 and 1968, he had Hoover set up a special FBI intelligence unit to spy on his political opponents, real and imaginary.

Former FBI agent Leo Clark, who headed the Bureau's office in Atlantic City, where the 1964 convention was held, told the Senate Watergate Committee that both electronic and physical surveillance was carried out by a special FBI team. The information thus obtained was transmitted to Johnson via a telephone line specially installed to bypass the White House switchboard.

Clark said that the data collected in this way concerned the activities of the Kennedys, the identities of the Congressmen visiting the hotel suite of Martin Luther King, and discussions of the convention delegates, including speculation about vice-presidential nominees.

One important use Johnson found for such highly personal information was that of intimidating legislators who did not always see things his way. It has been reported that he enjoyed placing a stack of FBI dossiers on his desk while subjecting vulnerable Congressmen to political arm twisting.[12]

After engaging in and encouraging this kind of spy government, Johnson said piously (albeit accurately):

"The worst thing in our society would be to not be able to pick up a phone for fear of its being tapped."

J. Edgar Hoover frequently made public statements to the same effect. Yet, it was recently learned that not only were illegal wiretaps used by the Bureau, but in one instance the tap was maintained for 25 years!

"People grew up and died and had babies, and this wiretap continued all this time," Prof. Leon Friedman of Hofstra University reported in testimony before a House Judiciary Committee on Civil Liberties.[13]

It is important to remember that the number of such incidents is not as important as the fact that they could occur at all. Once it is generally known amongst political leaders and legislators that secret dossiers containing derogatory information are being kept by federal agencies such as the FBI, IRS or CIA, the mere fact that these files exist is sufficient to inhibit the free exercise of their responsibilities to the electorate.

The possibility that the same "background data" could be transmitted to foreign police organizations should be cause for serious reflection. A detailed examination should be made of the entire operation of integrated federal information systems. Blackmail of important people in government is a favorite tool of the Soviet KGB and quite probably of other Communist secret agencies as well.

The proposed guidelines and administrative curbs aimed at limiting the collection, storage and release of sensitive information by the FBI are absolutely meaningless in today's James Bond world. The Bureau itself is a basic target of agent penetration for KGB men carrying out operations against the U.S.A. KGB training manual which came into the possession of Western security services, especially names the FBI, (along with U.S. cabinet members, diplomats and so on.), as one of the categories of espionage.

The instructions for Soviet secret agents include the recruitment of Americans as spies "on the basis of compromising materials." The textbook offers intelligence trainees the following guidance:

"When selecting candidates for recruitment on the basis of compromising materials, great importance is attached to information which, if revealed, could actually do serious harm to the person who is concealing it from those surrounding him."[6]

Testimony before the Senate committee investigating U.S. intelligence operations brought to light a case in which the mistress of an FBI agent was working for the KGB. When CIA learned from one of that agency's operatives in Moscow that the FBI was literally in bed with the KGB, Hoover's deputies broke into the woman's apartment, where they found FBI manuals, documents and reports.

The FBI agent was not prosecuted, however, because the ensuing publicity would adversely affect the widely accepted image of the incorruptible G-man, so carefully nutured over the years. Instead, the agent was allowed quietly to resign.

Another instance in which an FBI agent was believed to have passed confidential reports to the KGB occurred in 1961. He was fired on the basis of a minor technicality, and never brought to trial.[7]

There can be little doubt that some of the information the KGB is seeking from FBI files is available to them without the necessity of cloak-and-dagger intrigues. For example, if the KGB wanted to determine whether an American they had under surveillance abroad has ever been arrested for a certain offense, any of the many police forces around the world could obtain that individual's arrest record upon request from Interpol. ("It should be kept in mind," the KGB's secret training manual points out, "that the most important information that could compromise an American consists of data on the commission of serious crimes . . . and also information to the effect that he is a homosexual.")

Dispersion of data

Contrary to the impression FBI spokesmen seek to give Congressional committees and the general public — that information in their files has a very limited and supervised circulation

— there is documented evidence that it is, in fact, widely and irresponsibly disseminated.

When lawyers for the Church of Scientology, — the controversial religious movement long harrassed by official agencies — citing the Freedom of Information Act, demanded to see the files kept on that organization and its founder, they discovered that virtually every department of the Federal Government had information contributed by the FBI. Even the Energy Research and Development Administration admitted that they had six reports from the FBI in their files.

Without exception, the agencies refused to release the files under the FOI Act, stating that they had originated with the FBI and that the Bureau would have to give permission for their release.

The FBI, however, has proved very reluctant — indeed, at times, defiant — about allowing the subjects of its dossiers to review the contents of their own files. During a Congressional inspection tour of the new FBI building on February 24, 1975, U.S. Representative Robert F. Drinan stumbled upon a secret file the FBI was keeping on him. Current FBI Director Clarence M. Kelley, who promised the public "an open door" policy at the Bureau, stoutly resisted Drinan's demand that a summary of the dossier be turned over to him. Drinan later inserted into the *Congressional Record* an account of his tug-of-war with Director Kelley over the file. He accused Kelley of "acting in a lawless manner."

Kelley, who served under Hoover for 20 years and later as Kansas City police chief, was named Director of the Bureau by President Nixon in 1973. He has defended Hoover's policies, including the controversial Cointelpro, — secret programs of harrassment and "dirty tricks" directed against individuals and organizations Hoover considered extremist or undesirable.

Many fear that, while publicly calling for reform and deploring past abuses of the FBI, Kelley may continue some of the practices which brought those abuses about. At present he is clearly in a perfect position, as was Hoover, to define for himself the balance between needed confidentiality and exposure of the massive files that Bureau has built up. Whether the five Congressional bodies currently investigating the FBI will be able to deal with the problem satisfactorily is somewhat doubtful. Secrecy is a *sine qua non* of all police intelligence systems, and it is highly unlikely that new laws will change that. The FBI's (and indeed, every Federal agency's) past disregard for laws should make that clear.

In seeking to justify its refusal to release material from its confidential files, the FBI has expressed deep concern that to do so would violate the privacy of other persons. This is, in effect, to declare that it is more important to protect the identity of anonymous informers — many of them rumormongers, prostitutes, drug addicts, persons of unsound mind, and criminals under indictment — than to obey the well-settled principle of common law, that a person shall know of accusations against him and be faced openly by his accusers.

Even the course of justice in the U.S. is sometimes impeded by resistance of the FBI to disclosure of information vital to making a judicial decision. Not long ago, for example, a federal judge trying the case of two leaders of the American Indian Movement involved in the occupation of Wounded Knee angrily criticized the FBI because of inaccessible Bureau documents.

When U.S. District Court Judge Fred Nichol announced that he wanted to inspect the files intact in his chambers, Prosecutor R. D. Hurd said he did not think the FBI would agree to such an examination of the reports.

In an irate outburst, Judge Nichol declared: "I don't care what the FBI agrees or disagrees on. I used to think the FBI was one of the best bureaus to come down the pike, but now I think it has deteriorated, and I don't care how many FBI agents are in the courtroom to hear this."[14]

While thus guarding jealously the files the Bureau does not want released, the FBI itself disseminates by the thousands non-criminal reports containing unsifted data concerning the private affairs of individuals. A memorandum from Paul Wright, who headed up the notorious SS group within the IRS, notes that in the first 12 weeks of its operations, the Special Service Staff had received 581 FBI reports. "Each of these have a tremendous expansion effect on our files."

Wright added: "At least two technical people could keep occupied full time receiving FBI reports alone, evaluating them to determine whether committee actions should be undertaken, or the reports forwarded on for routing handling by other divisions."[15]

When the IRS was obliged to dismantle its SS program, these files, so generously provided by the FBI, were not destroyed but went into archives of Internal Revenue's intelligence division. Thus they can go on circulating through the extensive information network linking the various regulatory and law-enforcement agencies in the U.S. and — through Interpol — around the world.

Not only can the FBI never correct or update the material so widely dispersed, they do not attempt to do so. Even in the case of the computerized arrest records in the National Crime Information Center, there is no established procedure to insure that errors or incomplete data are regularly expunged or purged. The responsibility for assuring accuracy of information stored in the FBI data bank rests with the control terminal agency that entered it into the computer.

During the Dale Menard case, previously discussed, Beverly Ponder, special agent in charge of the FBI Identification Division was asked: "Does the FBI make any effort to obtain final dispositions where requests are received for arrest records before disseminating those arrest records?"

The agent's reply was: "We urge the contributors to obtain

final dispositions, but we don't go out and try to pick them up."[16]

That was an understatement. There is no evidence that the FBI ever made any real effort of any kind to encourage control agencies to enter follow-up dispositions of the arrests they put on record in the computer. Very few of them ever do so. Just how few is not known, since the Bureau has never compiled statistics on the question.

Commenting on the way the FBI tries to rationalize the irresponsibility of their record-keeping, a panel of three judges in the U.S. Court of Appeals who heard the Menard case (and found for Menard) had this to say:

"The FBI cannot take the position that it is a mere passive recipient of records received from others, when it in fact energizes those records by maintaining a system of criminal files and disseminating the criminal records widely, acting in effect as a step-up transformer that puts into the system a capacity for both good and harm."[17]

Menard's mother filed the suit only after she was unable to get either California authorities (who originated the report) or the FBI to expunge the record.

Even after the court ordered the record destroyed, the FBI merely moved it from a criminal to a non-criminal file, where it can still be retrieved.

Destruction of careers

An incomplete arrest record can sometimes destroy a career, since, among others, it is available to prospective employers. A striking example is the case of Dr. Doris Scott, 30-year-old social worker.

Dr. Scott, who earned a Ph.D. degree in sociology at the University of Florida, and a doctorate in divinity at Christian College, Fort Lauderdale, served as a member of the Committee on Child Welfare, set up by President Johnson.

The chain of events which was to culminate so unfortunately for Dr. Scott began in 1970 when an investigation for the California Department of Health Services visited her to inquire about a non-profit foundation by which Dr. Scott had formerly been employed. She told him what she knew of the organization and described the work she had done for them.

Two months later, the investigator returned, accompanied by an associate. The two agents demanded to see all the documents, including patients' records in Dr. Scott's possession, if they were concerned with a certain doctor who had worked at the foundation which employed the social worker.

Dr. Scott informed the investigators that she could not divulge patients' files which are protected by State law as being confidential. Thereupon the Health Department agent became abusive, and, according to Dr. Scott, threatened her as he was leaving with the words: "I'll get you for this! I know how to do it and I'll make you sorry!"

Another two months elapsed before the undercover agent reappeared at Dr. Scott's office, in the company of nine other persons, one of whom identified himself as an investigator for the District Attorney's office. He informed Dr. Scott that she was under arrest and mentioned six counts of grand theft. She said she had no idea what the charges referred to.

After being taken to the police station, where she was booked and fingerprinted, Dr. Scott was released on bail. She learned from newspaper stories the following day that she was accused of misusing state medical funds. In 1972, the court found her innocent of the changes.

Since that time, however, Dr. Scott has found it impossible to obtain employment. In her words: "Every time I go on an interview, I receive a tremendous initial acceptance. Then something always goes wrong. They tell me that I'm too old or they have found someone else or they just never call back. I have had to move three times since this horrible incident occurred. I have spent my life savings and I'm still in a sort of bondage."

It is reasonable to conclude that Dr. Scott's employment difficulties are directly related to her permanent arrest record, available for instant retrieval, stored in the FBI's National Criminal Information Center. Two years after Dr. Scott had been found not guilty of the charges against her, a printout of her NCIC file reports only that she was arrested on a felony warrant for six counts of grand theft. *Her acquittal is not shown.*

Dr. Scott's professional skills are the kind usually required by large institutions or social service departments of government, whether local, state or federal. These employers routinely check the FBI files to determine whether a prospective employee has a criminal record.

The gross injustice of the present system is too apparent to be seriously disputed.

Even if an enforceable means of purging and updating the NCIC records is found (and none is imminent at the time of this writing), it cannot be repeated to often that an unkown, but substantial, number of such incomplete and misleading reports have been passed to foreign agencies. These, together with other non-criminal personal histories, equally unreliable and damaging to the subjects, will remain beyond the reach of any U.S. law or regulation.

The question has been raised in respectable circles whether the FBI should continue to have control of the archives the Bureau has amassed. For instance, a three-year research study conducted under the auspices of the National Academy of Sciences recommended, among other things, that the storage and dissemination of summary criminal histories or "rap sheets" could be taken away from the FBI and placed in an independent agency. The agency established by "a clear legislative mandate to be a guardian institution," would be controlled by a board whose members would include representatives of the general public as well as law-enforcement officials.[18]

It is significant that this report was made in the pre-Watergate era, long before the recent disclosures of abuses by the FBI. Today the study and its conclusions deserve a second and more careful reading.

The whole issue of FBI autonomy is currently being studied by a team of six lawyers under the direction of U.S. Attorney General Edward H. Levi. The group will draft guidelines aimed at creating safeguards against future FBI misconduct. But unless the guidelines are eventually embodied in statutory law, they will be mere paper prohibitions. Control must be independent of the Bureau.

Of the many lessons to be learned from the national catharsis the U.S. has undergone since Watergate, one of the most important is that even the best of men, starting with the highest motives, may gradually lose their sense of balance and moral perspective if given power without accountability.

"We were sealed off from the outside world and the experiences and thinking of others from the very beginning," said William Sullivan. "We remained relatively so and steadily became inbred for 30 years."

Hoover created a private world in which he was all-powerful, a world insulated against corrective intrusions, one in which, as Sullivan adds, "the primacy of civil liberties on occasions gave way to expediency."

Thus without the insights that come from critical dialogue, Hoover drifted farther and farther from his professed principles and praiseworthy goals. His methods and personal conduct gradually came to resemble that of the criminal element he so often inveighed against.

The English poet, Edwin Muir, once described the process very well indeed:

"We have seen good men made evil wrangling with evil, straight minds grown crooked fighting crooked minds."

That was the sad story of J. Edgar Hoover.

> *"In the files of the Internal Revenue Service there are the most minute details of people's private affairs. Nobody has any secrets from the tax collector.*
> — U.S. News & World Report

9. *The IRS Connection*

In a previous chapter, note was taken of the fact that Interpol's operational centre in the U.S. — the National Central Bureau (NCB) — presently occupies six offices in the Treasury Building in Washington.[1]

The nerve-center of the IP bureau consists of two computer terminals which provide direct, automatic teletype access to two of the country's largest data banks. These are the FBI's National Crime Information Center and the Treasury Enforcement Communications System (TECS). The latter network, originally known as CADPIN (for Customs Automated

Data-Processing Intelligence), was started in April 1970, operating on an around-the-clock schedule.

Little known outside the law-enforcement fraternity, the TECS web, upon close inspection, is seen to be of impressive size. The circuitry branches out in all directions. It interfaces with the National Law Enforcement Telecommunications System (NLETS) thus linking it to criminal justice agencies in all 50 States. Most of these computerized law-enforcement systems have very loose or ineffective management controls over the data flowing through them.

Also plugged into the TECS network are the Bureau of Alcohol, Tobacco and Firearms; the U.S. Customs Service; the IRS Inspection Service, and the IRS Intelligence Division.

The latter agency is by far the most important in the present context. A veteran IRS agent who himself called it "an American Gestapo," described his role as "a combination of policeman and spy, and an outrageously powerful one at that . . . maybe, in fact, the most powerful in the country. There is no important piece of information concerning you that I am effectively forbidden to seek."[2]

The means employed by IRS special agents to obtain much of the personal information stored in the enormous IRS memory banks would be shocking to most people, if their moral nerve-endings had not already been reduced to insensibility by the atrocity stories that have emerged from our disintegrating political institutions.

A brief, informative look at this most sinister of all secret police systems in the United States is necessary, however, to appreciate the potential threat posed by its link-up with Interpol.

Almost from its inception, the IRS (formerly IRB) intelligence division has engaged in improper and at times flagrantly unconstitutional activities.

Elmer Irey, the investigative unit's first chief, has reported that "the Roosevelt administration made me go after Andy

Mellon" (meaning Andrew Mellon, prominent financier and former Secretary of the Treasury under FDR's predecessor, Herbert Hoover). Irey said the FBI had been given the assignment first, but "got tossed out of the grand jury room."

Irey and his undercover agents spent months working up the best case possible against Mellon, but they, too, failed. Mellon was found to be innocent of any wrongdoing.

Another prominent figure of a wholly different stripe, whom the Roosevelt hierarchy wanted the special agents to eliminate from the political scene was "that son-of-a-bitch from Louisiana," Huey Long. Henry Morgenthau, Jr., Roosevelt's Secretary of the Treasury, ordered the intelligence chief to push his investigation of Long and to report weekly on progress.[3]

The Government used the same means to cut down political boss Tom Pendergast of Missouri, when he became troublesome; and to jail assorted mobsters, abortionists, confidence men, drug traffickers, and so on, when police failed in their efforts to provide evidence to convict them.

In his memoirs, in fact, Irey leaves no doubt that from the outset, the IRS intelligence squad was regarded by many government officials (including himself) as a kind of all-purpose national police force, superior to the FBI.

For example, IRS special agents were brought into the Lindbergh kidnap case, where they acted as detectives trying to solve a crime not remotely connected with tax collection, and one clearly belonging to the purview of the FBI.

People generally applauded these operations as being in the public interest. What they did not, or perhaps could not, foresee, was that such a misuse of the tax agency — first against corrupt politicians or suspected criminals — would eventually be applied to all opponents of a regime in power. Allowed to proceed unchecked, it could become an instrument of general tyranny and personal revenge.

"What we cannot do in a courtroom via criminal prosecu-

tions to curtail the activities of some of these groups," wrote
White House aide Tom Huston, "IRS could do by administrative action."

Wholesale misconduct

The idea, inherent in the intelligence division of IRS from the
beginning, that, like the FBI, it is a law unto itself, has been
reinforced over the years by its agents' apparent immunity to
prosecution for their violations of law, — federal, State and
local.

Testimony before a Senate subcommittee on administrative
practice and precedure, in 1965, disclosed wholesale misconduct by IRS agents, who admitted practices that violate virtually every guarantee in the Bill of Rights. They had treated
with contempt the right of free speech, press, assembly and
religion and the security of the citizen's home, person, papers
and effects against unreasonable search and seizure.

The hearings produced evidence that some of the illegal
acts the IRS special agents had regularly engaged in were
more serious than any of those which put the Watergate
conspirators behind bars. They had: unlawfully tapped tele-
phones; picked locks and entered private offices and homes
without a warrant; planted bugs in citizen's homes, cars and
places of employment; criminally seized, opened and read
sealed first-class correspondence; stolen records and private
papers; installed hidden microphones and two-way mirrors
in IRS conference rooms to monitor privileged conversations
between taxpayers and their advisors; defied court orders;
and attended a funeral, where they took down the names of
all the mourners.

At the conclusion of the hearings, Senator Edward V. Long,
the committee chairman, summed up the situation in these
words:

"IRS has become morally corrupted by the enormous power with which we in Congress have unwisely entrusted it. Too often it acts like a Gestapo, preying upon defenseless citizens."[4]

In spite of the seriousness of these disclosures, the whole inquiry was given only token coverage in the media. The only alarm sounded was by what one IRS agent accurately described, as "isolated groups paddling their tiny rafts of advocacy on a vast sea of indifference . . . A few newspaper and magazine stories reported the results of the hearings, and then the subject faded from the headlines and disappeared. Nothing was done to diminish IRS's power or to give citizens weapons against the Gestapo personalities in IRS's ranks, and the Revenue Service today is the same as it has always been: much too powerful for its own or the country's good."[5]

Even the Long committee investigation did not bring to light the covert intelligence gathering and secret file-building in progress at the IRS. The concealment of these activities was so complete that as late as 1975, IRS Commissioner Donald Alexander said the operation, revealed during the Watergate fallout, had been in existence only since May 1973, when in fact it had begun more than 20 years earlier.

No sooner had Alexander made this statement than newly released documents showed that IRS had begun its prying into protected areas of the individual's personal life in 1951, when the agency reacted to the organized crime hearings held by Sen. Estes Kefauver. IRS that year set up a special unit for the declared purpose of gathering information on racketeers. But, as the documents clearly disclosed, while early guidelines were supposed to limit the operation strictly to organized crime, IRS officials later expanded the activity to cover a broader, less specialized area.

By 1969, the agency was ready to draft a new secret manual outlining procedures for collection of data to be stored in computerized intelligence files. The project was given the name of Intelligence Gathering and Retrieval System (IGRS). According to the manual, its purpose was "to provide an effective, uniform means for gathering, evaluating, cross-indexing and retrieving, on a district and national basis, intelligence data relating to individuals or entities involved in potential tax law violations."

This is plainly the definition of a full-scale spy system whose scope theoretically embraced the whole population, since under the vast, complex and constantly changing code of tax laws, anyone who has a tax liability could be considered a *potential* violator.

The fact is that much of the material collected by the IRS secret agents was not tax-related at all. It concerned such details as the drinking and sexual habits, political leanings and close associates of local politicians, celebrities and persons who had publicly protested against the present tax system.

The existence of the extensive IGRS computerized intelligence files came to public notice when a Government employee with access to the IRS centralized data bank in Detroit, circulated a five-page print-out segment of the IGRS program. A covering memorandum on official U.S. Government stationery was addressed to "Dear Concerned Party" and the text read:

"You are on this list. Some of your friends may be on it too and they would appreciate a copy from you." It was signed, "An American who believes in the United States Constitution."

The selective print-out of the IRS intelligence document index which followed, carried the names of 175 individuals, firms, churches and publications. The names were divided into more than a score of sections, about half of which bore the heading: "Tax Resister Project Index."

There were entries on such prominent persons as Walter H. Annenberg, former Ambassador to Britain; movie stars John

Wayne, Doris Day, Dean Martin, Frank Sinatra, and Jill St. John. Political figures indexed included Los Angeles Mayor Tom Bradley and US Representative Augustus Hawkins.

In addition to these entries, there were sections of the document which referred to "informants report," "wiretap," "organized crime in Australia," and "credit check."

Churches included

A separate section of the selective print-out was devoted to churches and religious organizations. Among them were the Church of Jesus Christ, the Worldwide Church of God, Church of Evangelism and the familiar target of all federal agencies, the Church of Scientology.

Under questioning by members of Congress, IRS officials said the IGRS files nationwide contained 465,442 names. Of these, 85,382 or about one-fifth, originated in the Los Angeles unit of IRS intelligence. No satisfactory explanation of the operation was ever forthcoming, and there is recent evidence that, despite IRS statements to the contrary, the programme is continuing.

The distance which exists, and no doubt will always exist, between the truth and statements made by IRS officials became apparent once again when the tax agency investigated itself and could find no wrongdoing in connection with the IGRS programme.

On March 13, 1975, IRS Commissioner Donald C. Alexander in testimony under oath before the House Subcommittee on Government Information and Individual Rights, said that none of the investigations he had ordered upon becoming Commissioner, turned up any serious cases of improper activity by the IRS.

The following day, the *Miami News* broke the story of Operation Leprechaun, a sordid and extensive spy activity carried on by IRS, in which paid female informants pried into the private lives and sexual habits of 30 prominent Florida citizens, including the State Attorney of Dade County, a Supreme Court justice and three federal judges.

One of the women, Elsa Suarez, a 33-year-old divorcee, said she had been ordered to "pick up all the dirt I could, maybe even go to bed with them." She said of the undertaking, "It was like a small CIA operation."

Her IRS superiors, Mrs. Suarez added, told her that they were interested mainly in the "sexual hangups" of the people she was assigned to watch, whom the intelligence officers assured her were all "bad actors," "that one was a homosexual, that others had mistresses."

She identified her immediate superior in the agency as John T. Harrison, and his superior as Thomas A. Lopez. Harrison provided her with photographs of her surveillance targets; a rented car on which the registration plates were changed weekly; and membership in the Jockey, Palm Bay and Mutiny Clubs — three of the most exclusive in Miami.

Mrs. Suarez — whose code name was Carmen — reported that during the Leprechaun operation, photographs were made of the home of a female Circuit Court judge, as well as of her pet monkey.

At one point, in the best KGB tradition, IRS agents discussed a plan to have a male agent "establish a relationship" with the judge. It was proposed to disable the judge's car and have an agent pretend that he had just happened by. He would fix her car and strike up an acquaintance.

Special Agent Harrison asked Mrs. Suarez to help recruit other undercover agents. She said she enlisted the services of two Cuban exiles, one of whom had worked with her previously when she was associated with the undercover operations of other Federal agencies, notably the Drug Enforcement Administration.

Harrison told her at one point during Operation Leprechaun that he had 31 such spies at work in the Miami area.

The IRS promised Mrs. Suarez a $20,000 annual pension for life, a new identity, and a home abroad if she were successful in "getting something on Gerstein" (State Attorney Richard Gerstein of Dade County, Fla.) She was receiving $200 a week, plus car expenses for her work.

After three months of largely unproductive effort, Mrs. Suarez told one of her contacts at IRS that she wanted to quit, "but the contact became very angry and threatened me and my children." After her disclosures to the press, Mrs. Suarez was given police protection . . .[6]

That such protection was necessary against the Mafia-type revenge of an agency of the U.S. federal government is in itself chilling proof that drastic reform is urgently needed.

Vindictiveness has for too long a time been a salient feature of the IRS intelligence division. Even the agency's own chief, Commissioner Alexander, has not been immune to covert attack. Some of the agents, disgruntled over Alexander's pledge to curb their reprehensible practices, informed the Church Select Committee on Intelligence Activities that the Commissioner had improperly halted an IRS investigation of certain U.S. citizens who may have filed false claims based on income-losing ventures in the Bahamas.

The truth was that Alexander, already under fire because of the agents' past crimes, cut short the Bahamas operation when he learned that an IRS secret agent had provided a Bahamian banker with a girl, and then while he was being intimately entertained by her, had removed from the banker's brief case and made copies of lists of American depositors.

In late June 1975, when the IRS master list of "enemies," was made public, Commissioner Alexander confessed that he was "distressed and discomfited" to find his own name on the list.

U.S. Representative Bella Abzug said on the floor of the House that just the day before the details of Operation Leprechaun were revealed, she had questioned John Olszewski, Director of the IRS Intelligence Division, if his agency had paid informants on its payroll. Speaking under oath, he had replied evasively:

"We do not necessarily have a man on payroll where he is receiving weekly or monthly payment."

Mrs. Abzug said that when the newspapers carried the story that a paid informer was in fact receiving a weekly salary — a direct refutation of Olszewski's sworn testimony, — she again asked the IRS official if the newspaper's allegations were true.

"I received the same vague assurances that the news stories were inaccurate or were exaggerations," Rep. Abzug said.

Warren Bates, IRS assistant commissioner for inspection, was likewise questioned at the same hearing. He declared:

"We looked at some of the activities of our group file, particularly those in one district. We found the same as Mr. Olszewski told you a few minutes ago. We do have managers and supervisors and employees who are importing information into the IGRS system. It is their judgment as to how they apply the guidelines issued to them. Undoubtedly the kind of information that goes in there — the sort of thing you talk about — can creep into those files."

Rep. Abzug tartly observed: "I hardly think, Mr. Speaker, that a concerted, long-term effort to pry into the lives of public officials can be passed off as information 'creeping' into the files."

"Either the Internal Revenue Service has the most inept leadership in the U.S. Government, or their senior officials lied to my subcommittee."

It would seem that the only "creeping" involved in Operation Leprechaun was that of IRS secret agents engaged in illegal acts. For example, one agent, Nelson Vega, admitted that he and a fellow operative named Roberto Novoa burglarized the office of a Republican congressional candidate in 1972. IRS officials airily dismissed the crime as "a lark."[7]

If this comment strikes the reader as being somewhat frivolous, he should bear in mind that *all* the answers given by federal agents to Congressional inquiries and to questions by the media, have been deliberately equivocal, partial, misleading or false.

A semantic wile

When IRS was asked by the *Miami News* to respond to the charges made by their erstwhile spy, the agency's public information officer told newsmen:

"I don't think that now we are in a position to deny that some of the information we got was definitely not tax-related. But when someone gives you a packet of information, it's apt to contain anything."

Of course, no stranger walked up to an IRS official on the street and gave him "a packet of information," nor slipped it anonymously into the agency's letter-box. But that was the impression the information specialist seemingly hoped to convey. It is, in fact, the kind of semantic sleight-of-hand that characterizes almost all official statements by Government spokesmen today.

Meanwhile, the illegal gathering of covert intelligence for the secret files that are the hall-mark of every police state, continues unchecked and unpunished.

Operation Leprechaun was not the only IRS programme of personal dossier-building to be uncovered in the recent national upheaval. During his testimony before the Senate Watergate Committee, John Dean alleged that certain members of the White House staff had set up a "Political Enemies Project," one of whose tactics was to use the IRS to harrass political foes of the Nixon administration.

In the course of his statement, Dean revealed the existence

of a secret Special Services Group within the tax agency, which was engaged in spying upon and collecting data about extremist organizations and individuals promoting dissident political views. He provided the committee with lists of high-priority targets which had been prepared by him and another White House aide.

As a result of Dean's disclosures, it was assumed, and so reported by the media, that the SS Group had been formed at the White House's request. This, however, was not the case. It was later learned that the spy squad had been operating since early August 1969. Originally it had been known as the Activist Organization Committee on Government Operations.

The stated purpose of the secret IRS unit when it was first created was to investigate 22 organizations categorized as extremist, militant or subversive, to determine whether they were violating tax laws.

The operation rapidly expanded to include many other organizations. One IRS memorandum stated that "it is expected that the Committee will function indefinitely." Another, dated July 24, 1969, declared, "One of our first problems is to define or to determine what kind of organization we are interested in. We have a general idea, *but we have no fixed limits."* (Emphasis added).

"What we are doing," explained an internal memo a few days later, "is trying to assemble all information available from within the Internal Revenue Service, from the Federal Bureau of Investigation, from the Department of Defense, from any other federal agency."

Paul H. Wright, who directed the information gathering facility, further clarified this objective when he wrote, in a briefing paper: "Existing I.R.S. information will be consolidated and substantially expanded from other sources and will over a period of time represent a massive intelligence file for us in initiating and facilitating I.R.S. actions."

Another IRS official document contains the admission: "From a strictly revenue standpoint, we may have little reason for establishing this Committee or for expending the time and effort which may be necessary, but we must do it."

"Red Seal" security precautions were imposed upon the group for fear its activities might become known to the American public. "We do not want the news media to be alerted to what we are attempting to do, or how we are operating," one memorandum cautioned, "because the disclosure of such information might embarrass the Administration or adversely affect the service operations in this area, or those of other federal agencies or Congressional committees."

In May 1970, IRS changed the name of the Activist Organization Committee to the Special Service Group, then to Special Service Staff, and expanded its surveillance "to include any other type of organization [besides activist] *or individual that may cause discredit or embarrassment to the Service.*" (Emphasis added).

It was at this point, in other words, that individuals and organizations exercising their Constitutional right to protest the U.S. tax system and to call for a reform or abolition of that system, became target for "special attention" by secret agents of the Internal Revenue Service.

The choice of the acronymn SS is not without psychological interest. It remains for future students of unconscious motivation in human behaviour to analyse the inner processes of the IRS officials who selected a designation which recalls the runic symbol of the Nazi elite corps, one of whose chief duties was also to compile secret dossiers on organizations and individuals who might cause discredit or embarrassment to the regime.

After Dean's testimony and under growing pressure from Congressional investigators, IRS Commissioner Donald C. Alexander announced to the media in August 1973, that the SS unit was being abolished.

As it turned out, the word "abolished" was not quite accurate in describing the agency's "phase-out, phase-in" operation which followed. Certainly, the SS organization as a separate group within the IRS, was disbanded. But as the directives issued to the personnel concerned with transitional activities made plain, the work was to be carried on as before. It was merely being transferred from the Special Service Staff to what Commissioner Alexander called "other components of the Service as a part of their regular enforcement activities." A task-force report was more specific: "There was general agreement that most of the functions performed by the Special Service Staff could be assumed by the Intelligence Division."

The report went on to recommend that "liaison both outside of and within the Service" be continued. Outside liaison would, in the main, consist of contacts with the FBI and certain "Hill" committees. "Data could be accumulated by Intelligence and integrated into their present tape program" [computerized data bank]. Intelligence gathering "should include the use of covert operations to discover subject matters."

The principal surveillance targets were to be tax resisters and tax protesters. In the press release announcing the dissolution of the SS staff, Alexander stated : "The IRS will continue to pay close attention to tax rebels."

The nation's press, however, which has an unenviable record in reporting IRS intelligence activities, continued to praise Commissioner Alexander for "abolishing" the Special Service Staff and all it stood for. The ongoing efforts of the IRS to equate tax protesters with major criminals, to be spied upon, recorded and harrassed, was never challenged, either in the media or on the "Hill."

The eve of America's Bicentenary, celebrating the greatest tax rebellion in history would seem to be an awkward time to move against citizens whose tax-rebel founding fathers had framed an incomparable document guaranteeing them the right of free speech and assembly, and to petition the government for redress of their grievances.

"A tax revolution"

There was word from inside the IRS, however, that agency officials were genuinely alarmed at the spreading dissatisfaction with the gross inequities of the whole tax system, as well as the police-state methods being used to enforce tax laws. A senior agency functionary declared privately: "It's really got beyond a tax-rebellion; it's a tax revolution."

To suppress the escalating wave of organized resistance, the IRS Intelligence Division, with the approval and active cooperation of several congressional committees (who, one would have thought, would be discussing tax *reforms*), has taken draconian and in some cases, frightening, action.

A special supplement (95G-50) to the Internal Revenue Service manual, headed *Tax Protesters*, spells out some of the measures to be taken. The over-all strategy is that of using a prominent protester as an example to frighten others into dropping out of their particular campaign.

"Nationally," says the manual, "the Intelligence Division has taken or is taking action against many violators who achieved self-prominence as tax protesters. We believe the publicity attending these enforcement actions has done much to deter others from embarking on similar courses of illegal action."

The point to be kept in mind here is that while non-compliance with tax law is an illegal action, tax protest is not. IRS is using the first to suppress the second. In one case cited in the manual as one of the agency's "successful prosecutions in the tax protest area," the amount of tax liability involved "amounted to about $5." But the defendant is identified as a member of the Fresno (California) based Tax Rebellion Committee and therefore his case could be used as an object lesson to other tax protesters. "After a discussion with the U.S. Attorney, it was decided that lack of a significant tax liability would not hinder the case." The trial judge sentenced the defendant to a year's imprisonment.

What most disturbs critics of this kind of administrative terrorism is that it is a method employed by the Soviet secret police. Carl J. Friedrich, an authority on the subject, writes that : "The psychological terror exercised by a group within a given society can, as a matter of fact, have a greater effect than physical terror, and the mere existence of a secret police, quite apart from what it does, suffices to maintain this feature."[9]

Almost two years after IRS publicly announced that the agency was halting non tax-related intelligence gathering, affidavits filed in federal court in Los Angeles quoted excerpts from IRS confidential files which revealed that agents were continuing to go far afield of legitimate tax-related investigations.

The affidavits, filed on behalf of income tax protester Terrance Oaks, brought to light the fact that between June 1972 and January 1975, IRS secret agents:

—Followed a number of tax protesters to church on several occasions and later handed in a report on the contents of the minister's sermons.

—Put into the IRS files the names, telephone numbers and car license numbers of all persons attending meetings of the Los Angeles Tax Rebellion Committee as well as other anti-income tax groups, irrespective of whether they were members of the organizations being spied upon.

—Included in their secret intelligence reports the name of any politician who attended a meeting of the protesters, or who simply had his name mentioned at such gatherings.[10]

To achieve a balanced perspective, these actions of the IRS secret police must be placed alongside an earlier public policy statement of the agency. On August 14, 1973, senior IRS official John P. Hanion announced:

"It is neither out intention nor desire to suppress dissent or to persecute individuals because they are critical of, or identified with groups critical of, the tax system or government policies."

The most frightening aspect of the federal government's response to dissent is the, as yet, limited, but increasing trend toward an even more ominous practice, familiar in accounts of KGB terror in Soviet Russia. That is the growing frequency of cases in which the defendant is sent to a psychiatric clinic "for a study of his mental condition."

For instance, among the "successful prosecutions" cited as guideline examples in the IRS Manual, is that of Jerome Daly, an attorney of Bloomington, Minnesota. As the case summary states, Daly had become very closely associated with another tax protester, Arthur J. Porth, who had "maintained a long history of opposition to the IRS." Apparently Daly had developed some Constitutional arguments against the present U.S. tax system — arguments the IRS regarded as a genuine threat.

Daly was indicted and tried for willful failure to file tax returns as required under Section 7203 of the Internal Revenue Code. A jury found him guilty of the offense, which is a misdemeanor, normally punishable by a short jail term. Under provisions of a federal law, aimed at determining the convicted person's suitability for probation, Daly was committed to the custody of the Attorney General "for a study of his mental condition." It was recommended that he be committed to, and that the study be conducted at, Sandstone (Minnesota) Federal Prison.

The same statute was used to send a San Diego woman for a 90-day psychiatric evaluation in Terminal Island Prison. She was Mrs. Barbara Hutchinson, a successful tax consultant and long time crusader for reform of the tax system. She had assisted John Barron, *Readers Digest* editor in researching the three-part series of articles on IRS tyranny, which attracted nationwide attention when it was published in 1966. She also became nationally prominent as founder of the Association of Concerned Taxpayers, an organization whose stated objective was to oppose the use of unconstitutional methods by the IRS. Mrs. Hutchinson had lectured widely and had appeared on radio and television programs across the country.

On the day following her acceptance as a witness to testify before a Senate subcommittee in Washington, Mrs. Hutchinson was informed that the IRS had taken legal steps to have her probation revoked. Her probation was the result of a prior case against her brought by the IRS.

Mrs. Hutchinson's attorney was able to get a postponement of her court appearance so whe could give her testimony at the Senate committee hearing. Just before she was scheduled to testify, an IRS agent reportedly went to the office of Senator Joseph Montoya, chairman of the subcommittee, and falsely informed him that Mrs. Hutchinson was under psychiatric treatment and evaluation and was unfit to testify. After ascertaining the true facts, Sen. Montoya ignored the IRS intervention and allowed Mrs. Hutchinson to testify.

The "psychiatric evaluation" which the IRS agent had said she was undergoing became a reality after Mrs. Hutchinson returned to San Diego. The dramatic account of her incarceration in the mental ward lies outside the scope of the present work; but it is a story that deserves the widest dissemination possible. What she describes is a Gulag Archipelago in miniature.

An increasing number of such disquieting cases — involving dissidents placed in psychiatric prisons — are accumulating in my files. Paragraphs (b) and (c) of the statute, (18 USC 4208) should come under the closest scrutiny of public-interest groups and appelate courts alike.

Extensive data collection

Cases such as those above are usually preceeded by months and sometimes years of surveillance and clandestine intelligence-gathering by IRS special agents. The undercover operations frequently involve liaison with other federal agencies, who add the reports and raw investigative data to their own files from which they can be and often are passed on to yet other agencies in the U.S. and abroad. These circulations contain personal information about people who were not themselves ever suspects in a given case, but merely friends, acquaintances, clients, or even spiritual counselors of the accused.

IRS officials stoutly maintain that sensitive information stored in the agency's immense data bank is hermetically sealed against disclosure to any person outside the Service, including their colleagues in the Interpol bureau. Given the arrogance and cynical duplicity that have characterized their behavior in the past, however, these pledges must be received with a certain amount of reservation.

As we shall show later, an Interpol report containing derogatory material about U.S. citizens was derived in part from IRS archives. Even when these case histories do not flow directly from the repository to the ultimate users they are released through multi access lines which serve several terminals simultaneously. Where they will reappear and in what form is a matter of conjecture.

A vast amount of information and misinformation is also circulated through the "buddy system," that is, by private memorandum or word-of-mouth among various federal departments and law-enforcement bodies.

In some respects this "informal" procedure is the most insidious kind of data trafficking of all, since it is often little more than gossip mongering. Opinions, rumors and prejudices are inserted into a growing and ever more widely dispersed report, alongside whatever hard facts it may contain.

A dramatic example of this kind of false dossier is one on file at the U.S. Department of Labor. Written as a memorandum, it is the report of an agent named Foley, who investigated the Church of Scientology "to form an opinion as to whether the body can be considered a bona fide religious organization for the purpose of alien employment certification.

Foley writes: "Contacted the US Dept. of Internal Revenue. Atty June Norris, Supervisor of Lawyers at Internal Revenue, 184-3843 and Charlotte Murphy (in charge of litigation in the case of the US vs the Church of Scientology) 184-4240 gave me a very comprehensive review of investigations made by the US Internal Revenue Dept as to the organization and operation of the Church of Scientology in the United States."

In the course of that conversation with IRS Attorneys Norris and Murphy, agent Foley says the following was reported:

1 - Mr. Hubbard, founder of the Church of Scientology "moved to England a few years ago after deserting his wife and children in Washington, D.C."

2 - "Mr. Hubbard has been the chief recipient of all contributions and profits from this organization."

3 - "There is evidence that LSD and perhaps other drugs are widely used by the members while assembled."

4 - "There is evidence that an initiation ceremony is held for all new members at which time an electric shock is administered to them."

5 - "There is evidence that members of several families in different parts of the U.S. have been shot, but not killed [sic!] by unknown persons because they have objected to their teen-age children becoming members."

Each of the "facts" recited in the above report is, in fact, an outright falsehood, and each constitutes a gross libel of the church, its founder, and its members.

Nevertheless, some of the false allegations contained in it, and in others like it, were incorporated into an FBI report, which was then passed to Scotland Yard and from Scotland Yard to Interpol and from Interpol to a West German governmental agency, thence to a psychiatric institute whose directors leaked it to the European press.

After it was revealed that the Church of Scientology was on the IRS enemies list, a federal judge in Honolulu, who was hearing a suit brought against the U.S. Government by the Scientologists, issued a restraining order forbidding any federal agency to destroy the secret files they had on the church or anyone connected with the church. But while these dossiers may not have been put through the shredder, to date a considerable number of them have remained buried from sight in the various secret archives of the Government. Others, like the arrow of Longfellow's famous poem, have been shot into the air, to fall to earth we know not where. Perhaps long, long afterward, they too will be found in an oak — a "dead drop" of the KGB.

> *"Here in Britain, we are developing a monitoring system which would be the envy of every dictator from Genghis Khan to Hitler."*
>
> — Hugh Macpherson (London *Telegraph*)

10. *Squad 3: Interpol in Britain*

Unlike the situation in the United States, in Britain there was never any doubt about where Interpol belonged in the country's administrative structure. The reason is that no one was asked.

Ronald Howe, British member of the postwar executive committee which reorganized Interpol, simply decided to incorporate the I.C.P.C. as a separate unit within Scotland Yard's Criminal Investigation Department, of which he was the chief officer.

The matter never came before the Parliament and therefore

was never debated; nor was any kind of formal agreement ratified by that body. Likewise, there is no evidence that the British Home Office, which exercises control over the Metropolitan Police (i.e., Scotland Yard) ever authorized the establishment of an Interpol office in Britain. Acting on his own initiative, Howe brought it home, planted it in the Yard, and it grew until today it is one of the three largest in the world.

Apparently, under the vague and ambiguous statutes defining the powers and functions of the police in Britain prior to 1964, a unilateral action of this kind was legal.

Today, among the ten squads that comprise Scotland Yard's specialist branch known as C-1, (the oldest in the CID), Squad 3 acts as Interpol agent for all the police forces of England, Scotland, Wales and Northern Ireland. Included in the Interpol staff of 28 persons are 15 civilians and 13 detective constables and sargents. During 1973, a typical year, they handled 30,000 requests for information.

In addition to paying the costs of Interpol's London-based operation, Britain is assessed 354,000 Swiss francs (£60,000) each year for membership in the international organization.

As would be expected, there is an established liaison between Interpol's London office and police forces on the Continent, not only through regular Interpol channels, but on an unofficial basis as well. As one writer observed, if the Yard wants information about a Spaniard, for example, that it would be improper to request directly from Interpol, "Interpol meetings and the International Police Association encourage friendships, and doubtless someone can ring up old Juan in Barcelona to find out."[1]

There is even closer cooperation, of course, between Squad 3 and other units of the Yard's Criminal Investigation Department. This is especially true in the case of those that deal with such matters as forgery of bank notes, extradition and fugitive offenders, the Drugs Squad, the Criminal Record Office, and the Fingerprint Branch. There is also a close working relationship with Criminal Intelligence (C-II), although not a great deal is known about it, owing to the secrecy surrounding that branch of the CID.

In fact, the functions not only of the police, but of virtually every administrative department of the British Government are to a greater or less extent, cloaked in secrecy, so far as the general public is concerned.

In every country, secrecy is the bureaucratic way of life, but in Britain it has the sanction and protection of law. For the past 65 years, journalists, historians, and reformers have been thwarted in their efforts to know what goes on inside their government owing to provisions of a statute known as the Official Secrets Act.

Passed in 1911 during a time of spy hysteria preceding World War I, it was intended to provide the legal means of dealing with espionage, the wrongful disclosure of information affecting the safety and security of the State. It was a simple "breach of official trust" act which made the communication, but not the receipt, of official data an offense.

In 1920, however, the Act was expanded and the highly restrictive Section 2 added, making it a crime to *receive* knowledge of state matters unless the recipient could show that such information was passed to him "contrary to his desire."

Even worse, the amending Act of 1920 defines the protected material by the all-embracing term of "safety or *interests* of the State." As a legal guidebook for journalists observes, "it can certainly cover all 'classified' material emanating from a Government department, and all state employees are required to sign a declaration that they will not communicate any communication they acquire through that employment unless expressly authorized to do so."[2] The ban continues in effect after retirement or leaving government service.

Provisions of the 1920 Act also make it an offense to solicit, incite or endeavour to persuade another person to divulge official secrets.

A threat to newsmen

The foregoing interdictions would seem to effectively place investigative reporters in a legal straightjacket, and of course, they do. But another amendment to the Act in 1939 restricts even further, if that is possible, the activities of the press. Section 6, as amended, provides that if a chief officer of police has reasonable ground for suspecting that a violation of the Official Secrets Act has occurred, he may apply to the Home Secretary for permission to interrogate the journalist regarding his sources of information (if a story has been published) or any relevant information, even if it hasn't left his typewriter. Anyone who fails to comply with the requirement or gives false information, is guilty of a misdemeanour.

Paradoxically, after insulating every department of government from public scrutiny, the British spend £30,000,000 ($60,000,000) a year to operate an official information service. But as one London newsman complained, its function appears to be to obstruct any attempt by the people to find out what is really going on behind the majestic closed doors.

Malcolm Stuart of the London *Daily Mail* wrote recently that rare access to one of the elite band of top government officials in Britain involves lengthy applications. When granted, the interview is conducted in the presence of a Government public relations representative who records every word.

"What is said is so bland, it is frequently useless, and the briefing is usually 'unattributable' anyway."

Stuart comments that the Home Office (which has direct control of Scotland Yard) is one of the two most consistently secretive ministries in government.

His observation is correct, and what he says of all his country's rulers is doubly true of the Home Secretary and the functionaries who work under him:

"It is their insolence which is ultimately unforgiveable; their conviction that they have the right to decide what we ordinary mortals should know about the way they manage our affairs.

"They have been corrupted by their own conceit as surely as others are corrupted by money and just as surely have injured democracy. The time has come to call them out."[3]

As this writer's stirring words so eloquently attest, there is a groundswell of informed opinion in England which is demanding an end to the kind of in-camera government that is embodied in provisions of the Official Secrets Act.

Unfortunately, the strongest winds of change seem to be blowing through the media and intellectual forums rather than through the corridors of power.

While it is true that the Government have set up various committees to study the problem, and have issued reports and White Papers recommending legislation that would make the citizen's affairs more private and the ministries' affairs more public, no measures to effect this change have yet been brought before the Parliament.

Aware of the growing public interest in the issue, the Home Office in February 1976 announced that an interdepartmental study group of senior civil servants had been set up to consider whether fundamental human rights need better protection under the law.

The fact that the committee's point of departure was to *consider whether* human rights need better protection is a clear enough indication of the kind of results to be expected from the enquiry. A top Home Office official said it might eventually lead to publication of a Green Paper, to promote public discussion.

Thus, given the leisurely pace at which the official push toward reform is moving, by the time the needed legislation is passed, Britons may find that electronic technology has preempted their efforts.

There are already 220 computer-based "tasks" being performed by Her Majesty's central government, which involve the use of sensitive personal information about people. Some of this material is drawn from sources which are far from reliable as to accuracy, and questionable as to propriety.

A British physician, Dr. John Linklater, MBE, recently cited a striking example of this kind of record-keeping. Mrs. Carol Parris, aged 25, by means unknown had come into possession of her personal dossier, kept by the Government's social security office. She found that it contained, among other thing, a derogatory psychiatric diagnosis made by the counter clerks who interviewed her in the agency's office.

According to their assessment, she had sexual difficulties, a father fixation, and a neurosis which called for medical treatment. The file further stated that she had not had sexual intercourse for a year.

When the incident was reported in the press, a spokesman for the social security department defended these comments, implying that they were justified because interviewers were trained to pass judgment on the psychiatric state of anyone making an application for benefits.

Dr. Linklater noted that department officials appeared to be far more concerned with discovering how Mrs. Parris obtained the file than with the contents.

Informed sources predict that in the immediate future all important information storage and retrieval by central and local government in Britain will be carried out by electronic data processing.

It is in the area of computerized police intelligence and criminal information, however, that the greatest strides are being made.

Broad implications

A Police National Computer System giving local forces throughout the United Kingdom access to selected central records has already gone into operation under the direction of the Home Office, together with Scotland Yard.

Officials responsible for the centre's operation have shown their customary reluctance to reveal details concerning it, but sufficient information has emerged in one way or another to give an accurate general picture of the system.

At the heart of the installation is a £5 million ($10,000,000) twin Burroughs computer. The estimated total cost of the system, including hardware, staff and running expenses to 1980 is between £30 million and £40 million ($60,000,000 and $80,000,000).

When fully operational, it will be the largest "real-time" immediate-response system of its kind in Europe. By late 1970, 1000 terminals in regional crime squad offices and main force areas in Britain will be plugged into it.

Initially, the central files were set up to handle information covering stolen vehicles and property, missing and wanted persons, an index of Scotland Yard's fingerprint file, and a complete check-list of all registered owners of motor vehicles.

Now, the system is being expanded to include scene-of-crime investigative reports, non-police information derived from Department of Environment records stored in the licensing computer in Swansea; and details of disqualified drivers and persons subject to suspended sentences.

Most important of all, the new Police National Computer is taking over the massive criminal intelligence files of Scotland Yard. According to the *Police Review*, a publication for law-enforcement personnel, specially appointed collators in most police divisions are also busy bringing together the data they want put into the bank.

"Much of the information," the *Review* explains, "is personal detail of a suspect, his family, associates, and way of life, and although it may seem to trespass on the freedom of the individual, it is the bread and butter of successful police-manship."[4]

The article boasted that the computer system "is to be far more comprehensive than any other computerized intelligence service in the world." This statement echoed an affirmation made earlier in almost identical words by Lord Stonham.[5]

Up to the present time, Scotland Yard has maintained dossiers on slightly more than 2,000,000 persons; but with the advent of the National Police Computer, the number can be expected to increase exponentially. The demand for more information always grows with the system's capacity to store and manipulate it.

What, exactly, do the files contain?

First, the criminal record gives the subject's name, offenses, convictions, courts where sentenced, and dates. Accompanying this is another "descriptive form," also bearing the offender's name, age, address, description of physical appearance when arrested, circumstances of arrest, and a photograph.

There is, as well, an "antecedents sheet," which has been characterized as voluminous, discursive and subtle. It is likewise often inaccurate, intrusive and incomplete — in a word, defamatory. It provides a brief personal history of the subject, dealing not only with matters associated with his crime but also such things as his family life, finances, medical history, last-known wage rate, any hire purchase, *and his associates*.

"An experienced police officer, on reviewing an antecedents sheet richly supplied with these kinds of information, can often form highly sophisticated judgments of the criminal's likely future movements and activities. Likewise, the police use information generated in the course of 'stop checks' in subtle ways that can involve highly discretionary decision making. The details of past convictions, for example, may make the difference between arresting a suspect or bidding him good evening . . . . ."[6]

There is, in fact, no statutory limitation restricting the type nor amount of information about people that police can put into their files. At present that decision rests solely with the Home Office and with the police themselves. The original legislation — the Habitual Criminal Act of 1869 — under which the files system originated, required only that the Metropolitan Police maintain a registry of persons *convicted* of crime in England. It provided no specific legal authority for establishing integrated archives to squirrel away extensive dossiers containing the life details of ever larger areas of the population.

With the alarming rise in the crime rate, however, especially crimes of violence and disruption that at times have threatened the very existence of an orderly society, police have felt the need for more readily accessible information to control it. This is a legitimate need and, if it could be confined to the sphere of criminal activity, would provoke no opposition from libertarians.

Eye of the system

Unfortunately, the trend is toward a total surveillance situation. As the British writer Glyn Jones observed, "this enormous accession of computer power could become the eye of a system for the scrutiny and control of the non criminal."[7]

The law-enforcement file-keepers are moving relentlessly in that direction. When questioned by the more thoughtful elements in society, who are worried about the eventual import of such systems, they become petulant and defensive or, more commonly, outright deceptive.

Speaking for the Home Secretary, Lord Harris replied to a query from Arthur Lewis, M.P., concerning the information flow from the new police computer: "There is no question of the Police National Computer being linked to a world-wide network of police computers via Interpol, nor is there any intention of linking the Department of Health and Social Security to the police computer."

There is, as a matter of fact, a serious question about both these issues. Lord Harris and his colleagues may have no *intention* of such a link-up, but historical patterns offer persuasive evidence that such a coupling will almost certainly occur. The agents who control the various data banks around the world have already joined hands in an informal exchange of intelligence, some of it proscribed by law. In the interest of greater speed and efficiency it would seem inevitable that they would follow the course they felt to be best, as they have done in the past, and public opinion be damned.

If the situation were otherwise, there would be no need for the secrecy which surrounds the operation, nor of the misleading and sometimes false statements that regularly issue from the official citadels.

Despite annoyed denials by government officials, it is now well-known that sensitive information about individuals, including non-criminals, is made available to people who have no legal right to it.

James B. Rule, a responsible scholar and researcher, who made a study of public surveillance systems in Britain, reports a mixed experience in dealing with the Home Office. It involved both limited cooperation and attempted duplicity. "One unacceptable act," he wrote, "was the denial by senior Home Office officials, that the police routinely report criminal record information to outside agencies. Those who made this denial certainly knew better, and the discussion on this point has made it clear that *the provision of such information is both routine and extensive.*"[8] (Emphasis added.)

Another source of anxiety for those concerned with civil liberty is the growing emphasis by law-enforcement agencies on pre-criminal determent, still commonly called crime prevention.

The idea that police should concern themselves with *potential* offenders as well as criminals who have broken the law is not a recent one.

During the creation of the Metropolitan Police in 1829, Charles Rowan and Richard Mayne, the Yard's first two Commissioners, declared that "the primary object of an efficient police force is the *prevention* of crime. "To this great end every effort of the police is to be directed. The security of person and property, the preservation of public tranquility and all other objects of the police establishment will thus be better effected than by the detection and punishment of the offender *after* he has succeeded in committing the crime . . . . Officers and police constables should endeavour to distinguish themselves by such *vigilance* and activity as may render it impossible for anyone to commit a crime within that portion of the town under their charge."[9]

Every law-abiding person is, of course, whole-heartedly in favour of crime prevention. Today, however, this no longer means that a police constable on his rounds keeps an eye peeled for suspicious behaviour or unusual circumstances that require on-the-spot investigation.

It means, rather, the gradual development of a mass surveillance system which can have but one ultimate result — the control of criminals by controlling everyone in society. The collection, exchange and manipulation of computerized data about individuals and groups can indeed provide intelligence that will enable police to forestall much of the crime and violence that afflicts present-day life. It appears to be a highly efficient tool and that is why the authorities are determined to keep it and to expand its use.

Defenders of the preventive-action concept argue that only "persons of interest" are watched and recorded. But we have already reviewed evidence that not only the allegedly dangerous person is spied upon, but also his family, friends, associates, and so on. The unverified data about them is put into permanent files and widely disseminated without their knowledge or consent.

Moreover, the theory that crime can be prevented by identifying the potential authors of future offenses, has been extended to embrace that unreliable and dangerous instrument, the psychiatric report.

In America — the seedbed of despotic ideas in our time — a programme is already in operation, in which children in the early years of their schooling are singled out as "the possible killers and robbers of the future." Even young tots of kindergarten age are watched for aberrant behaviour which might point to the "pre-delinquent." Information regarding the little black sheep is fed into a computerized criminal records file for future retrieval.

Parents are not informed that their child is the subject of a pre-delinquent file. Perhaps the first they will learn of it is when, as a boisterous teen-ager he or she is stopped for a traffic violation and the police query will be answered in seconds with the information that the subject was a pre-delinquent in school.

In California, where the first demonstration studies of this technique are being carried out, the agencies involved are making efforts to comouflage the activity. The projects, which are financed by state and federal funds, are disguised by such euphemistic labels as "Behaviour Assessment," "Simplified Analytical Methods of Behaviour Systematization," and "Correctionetics."

Asked to explain what the latter term meant, a spokesman for the California Council on Criminal Justice, which sponsors it, said it designated "a plan to computerize and centralize all juvenile records, including information on psychiatric treatment."

A Los Angeles news service reported that grants totalling $2 million were given to an organization known as the California Technical Research Foundation to develop, among other things, "early detection measuring devices for the propensity of a person to riot or commit a criminal act."[10]

Privately, some educators have expressed misgivings about the scheme. One was quoted as saying: "The kids who are picked for the programme may not be pre-delinquent at all. They just might be some kids who have a personality clash with their teacher — and for that they get a record for life and submission to some 1984 brain machines."

In Britain, *Where*, the magazine for parents, revealed that many English schools keep secret card-files on small children.

The article reported that in Dorset, the cards are made available for inspection by anyone; in Flintshire, they are shown to prospective employers. Elsewhere, such records have been passed along to the police.

In a typical file, a 10-year-old boy was described as having "dirty sexual habits"; and a girl in primary school was characterised as having "vicious tendencies."

Paul McNamee, the teacher who wrote the article in *Where*, quoted a headmaster as saying: "What is little better than idle tittle-tattle, ignorance and gossip is passed about as if it were Holy Writ."

McNamee said he knew teachers who, because they refused to keep secret records on children, "have been slighted, threatened, and denied promotion."

Britain's National Health Service plans to start the individual's computerized life history even earlier. One new system being prepared by the NHS is called the Multipurpose Child Surveillance computer record, of which the designers say: "In general, a computer-held record is established with the birth of the child."[11]

"Persons of interest"

Interpol, it appears, would also like to see a pre-delinquent programme put into operation worldwide. In the organization's official publication, *International Criminal Police Review*,

Dr. Julien Severy of the Antwerp Police Studies Centre proposes:

"Mental deficiency should be diagnosed during childhood and those suffering from it should be given suitable training and kept under some form of control."

It is important to realize that in adult as well as juvenile crime prevention, the eventual purpose of the cummulative records on "persons of interest" must be some form of action taken to deter the criminal-to-be from committing an offense.

It is but a short step from surveying potential law violators to placing them under preventive arrest.

That was the step taken by Heinrich Himmler the moment he was firmly in charge of the police. In early 1937 he ordered all offices of the KRIPO (criminal police) in Germany to compile a list of criminals and "dangerous persons" in their areas and to assign a number to each. "When the time comes," the order declared, "only the list number of the criminals concerned will be telegraphically transmitted."

The time came only a month later, when the suspects were taken into "preventive police custody" and delivered to concentration camps at Sachsenhausen, Sachsenburg, Lichtenburg and Dachau.

As Heinz Hoehne points out, the German police had no legal authority to place anyone under preventive arrest. As in the case of Britain or the United States today, this method of crime suppression was embodied in no law. But Dr. Werner Best, the SS legal expert, soon came up with an argument for the theory and the courts did not reject it.

The Nazi security police (including Interpol at that period) labelled whole categories of persons "anti-social malefactors" and placed them under preventive arrest. "So a process began in which the community was treated like a nursery garden where the ill-grown shoot has to be 'plucked out' and 'rooted out' at regular intervals."[12]

Another aspect of the "investigation before the act" procedure which has stirred real concern among British civil rights groups is the temptation it provides for what, in police jargon is called a "fit-up," or a "stitch-up," meaning a deliberately false report concocted to support an arrest.

"If the tendency is to catch a person before he 'does the deed,' large amounts of evidence are needed. So why not arrange the evidence?"[13]

During the past few years there have been a number of allegations reported in the press of senior police planting incorrect or ambiguous data in their files.

In a cummulative record, it is surprisingly easy to give a wholly inaccurate picture of an individual's character, even without resorting to outright lies, as anyone who has ever read his own dossier from the confidential files is aware.

In the course of a Parliamentary debate on the Data Surveillance Bill in 1969, (which failed to pass, incidentally), Lord Ritchie-Calder drew attention to this risk, inherent in all biographical documentation. He said that during the last war, he accidentally gained access to his own police dossier, which he read with growing fascination. He kept thinking, "What a sinister, exciting character this Calder must have been! I wish I had known him."

He added: "One episode, the real circumstances of which I had practically forgotten because they were so unimportant, assumed the glamour and deviousness of a really exciting James Bond. But I did not recognize myself, and could not have given completely simple explanations of incidents which had acquired suspicious significance."[14]

Such information — concerning character traits, physical and mental health, personal habits and so on — are nothing more than hasty value judgements made by unqualified individuals. Yet, given the right circumstances in an individual's life, any one of them may become momentous because it represents official opinion.

Any recorded statement of persons in authority, if it is

derogatory, can have serious consequences when passed on as an Interpol circulation, for example.

Something of the kind occurred in the Cartland murder case in 1973.

John Cartland, a former British intelligence agent, was brutally hacked to death with an axe while camped on a lonely roadside in Southern France, where he was on holiday with his 29-year-old son, Jeremy.

Even though Jeremy Cartland was hospitalized with wounds that he, too, received during the bloody incident, French police decided that they were self-inflicted and that he was his father's murderer.

For six hours, according to Cartland, the French detectives interrogated him. "They sat on either side of me and kept nudging me in the stomach, 'accidentally' hitting my wounds. The lights blazed down on me. I had to ask for water. They said I was homosexual. They said I was a sadist. On and on, over and over again. They took away my clothes and all my possessions."

When Cartland was brought before a French magistrate in Aix-en-Provence, the examining judge produced a statement from Interpol alleging that Jeremy Cartland was "a liar and not to be trusted."

Such, the report said, was the professional judgement of Prof. James Cameron, the Home Office pathologist who had examined Cartland in London and afterward had stated that opinion to Scotland Yard. The Yard had then passed it on to Interpol and Interpol had given it to the French police.

Prof. Cameron subsequently denied having made the statement — at least in the terms attributed to him by Interpol. He declared that he had not made a written report, and "liar is not a term I would use. I am not a psychiatrist."[15]

Cartland was eventually cleared, but only after a great deal of personal anguish and the expenditure of several thousand pounds of legal fees. He reportedly talked of suing Interpol for introducing false evidence into his preliminary trial at Aix-en-Provence; but in the end, apparently his experience with the French legal machinery and the advice of his counsel dissuaded him from taking that action.

The full contents of the report sent from Scotland Yard to Interpol Paris was never disclosed. Nor is it likely that Jeremy Cartland will ever know what other defamatory material is included in his dossier at the Yard. While willing and ready to share the file with the police of the 122 member countries of Interpol, Scotland Yard officials refuse to allow anyone to see his own file or to correct the misinformation in it.

A specious argument

Commenting on this issue, Lord Harris employed the same specious argument that had been used previously by FBI spokesmen in the U.S. He said:

"As for the suggestion that individuals should be able 'to view their files and make documented corrections,' one practical objection comes to mind immediately and that is the difficulty of establishing beyond doubt that a person asking for a copy of a police record was the person entitled to have it."[16]

Such difficulty of identification does not seem to extend to other agencies seeking access to the individual's file. There is no statute effectively limiting the circulation of information in the Yard's confidential records. The insistence of Home Office officials that only law-enforcement agencies that can show a need to know are given data must be weighed against the fact that Scotland Yard reports surface in some odd places.

The Freedom of Information Act in the United States, for example, has provided a legal instrument for prying open files of various regulatory departments of the Government, which contained memoranda from Scotland Yard. By way of illustration: the U.S. Food and Drug Administration, the Internal Revenue Service, the U.S. Customs, the Bureau of Economic Affairs, even the Department of Labour have all quoted from or had in hand reports from the Yard.

To shrug off the responsibility by asserting that these agencies did not get their information *directly* from the Yard or from Interpol does not confer absolution on the original disseminators. None of the memoranda in question — or almost none — is more than one remove from the source. It would be a simple matter to discipline the secondary communicator.

Instead, senior officials at the Yard have developed close liaison with the worst offenders in the matter of circulating intrusive personal information about people, most of it unverified and some of it slanderous.

It is not generally known, for instance, that part of the function of one of the ten squads in Scotland Yard's CI is to maintain a close working relationship with the American Embassy in London.

This activity must be considered while keeping in mind the fact that U.S. Embassies the world over, but particularly those of London and Paris are staffed with an extraordinary number of undercover agents working for the CIA, IRS, U.S. Customs, Drug Enforcement Agency and others.

The embassies routinely circulate memoranda called Airgrams, which often contain details of people's private lives. The distribution list of one of these typical communications will reveal the scope of their dissemination.

Airgram A-150, dated January 29, 1969, was sent from the U.S. Embassy in London to the following terminals (the figures opposite each name indicate the number of copies sent to that recipient):

Bureau of European Affairs	6
Records Management, Records Office	1
Office of Intelligence and Research	5

Bureau of Economic Affairs	4
U.S. Undersecretary For Political Affairs	2
Bureau of International Organizations	5
Legal Advisor — State Department	3
U.S. Secretary of State	1
Passport Office, — Bureau of Security and Consular Affairs	1
SCA (State Department)	1
Visa Office	1
U.S. Air Force Intelligence	5
U.S. Army Intelligence	3
CIA	20
U.S. Navy	5
Secretary of Defense	34
U.S. Information Agency	10
National Security Agency	3
Health, Education and Welfare	7
U.S. Department of Justice	1
National Security Council	6
FBI	1
Total	125

The absence of both Scotland Yard and Interpol from the distribution list of this particular circulation may be due to the fact that the material contained in the circulation was already in their files. Also the liaison between the Yard and the U.S. Embassy is carried out through different channels of communication.

Watchdogs on chains

Responding to increased pressure by the media and by a handful of Parliamentarians concerned with the issue, the British Government on December 16, 1975 announced plans for setting up a computer watchdog committee.

It was a first step, declared a Home Office White Paper, toward framing new laws to protect the privacy of individuals, as more and more personal details about people are fed into computer systems.

Of course, as a Chinese proverb suggests, a first step may be the start of a 1000-mile journey.

The cautious replies given by a Home Office junior minister, Alex Lyon, to questions put to him by a BBC interviewer make it clear that the Government are not preparing for a 40-yard dash.

When asked by the BBC reporter, "What are the guidelines you're laying down to protect the privacy of the individual?," the Home Office spokesman said:

"There are a substantial number of them: that the individual should be given *some kind* of information about what is held about him on the computer; that he should have the right to know *in general terms* what the information is required for; and that it shouldn't be used beyond that . . ." (Emphasis added).

The junior minister agreed with the assertion made in the White Paper that fears about the improper use of computers in the public [that is, official] sector are not justified by present practice. "I think everybody is agreed that the danger is not at present — it's in the future."

Dr. Joseph Hanlon, an authority on computer privacy, who was interviewed by BBC during the same broadcast, accurately summed up the situation in these words:

"The Home Office report sets up a data protection committee, which is simply a study committee which, in a year to a year and a half, will report back with proposals to set up a statutory data protection authority. So, we're at least three years away from any serious legislation, and it has already been three years since this sort of thing was proposed.

"In essence, the Home Office has just said, we won't do anything for awhile."

In the meantime, information systems are one of the few real growth industries in Britain.

> *"Data banks have been set up by various
> countries. Why not do the same on an in-
> ternational basis?"*
>
> — Jean Nepote
> (Secretary General of Interpol)

11. *The Orwellian Dream*

If Interpol is to survive during the coming decades as an
international reservoir of police intelligence, the organization
has no choice but to computerize its files.

This fact is so obvious that it need not be pressed. Interpol's
executive committee recognized the situation several years
ago and have been quietly at work on the problem since then.

Jean Nepote, the Secretary General, who is in charge of
Interpol's global operations, first proposed the idea of an
international data bank to the General Assembly in 1972.

"True, the Interpol machinery now makes it possible for

police forces to exchange information rapidly, but we have to admit that it was not designed to answer a massive number of enquiries within a matter of minutes. But this is precisely what is needed by the police officers who are in direct contact with crime in the streets, or in their offices. When they question a person, confirmation of his replies must not — indeed, cannot — wait. Computers can provide the answer to this problem."

The delegates responded with enthusiasm and a working party composed of computer experts from 12 countries was set up to make an in-depth study of the project.

The first conclusion to emerge from the analysis was that half-measures would be useless. That is to say, it would not be economically feasible merely to computerize the files at Paris-St Cloud unless there are terminals at least in the principal member countries.

The project envisions the setting up of a network that, on an international level, would be comparable to the FBI National Crime Information Centre in Washington.

Some of the foremost advisors to the study panel have been specialists from the U.S. Treasury Department. They have explained the type of equipment used by the U.S. Secret Service and the Customs Department, and have discussed their methods, difficulties, and security problems.

If the French government follows an earlier precedent, they may well provide a substantial portion of the funds eventually needed to establish the data processing system.

During the postwar period, after Paris was made the operational centre of Interpol, the organization was dependent upon the generosity of the host country to establish its facilities and pay a large part of its running expenses. As late as 1952, France contributed 72% of Interpol's annual budget, as compared to Britain's payment of only 2%.

In 1953, the 22nd General Assembly was informed that "we have obtained from the French government the exceptional grant of 15,000,000 French francs to improve radio transmissions. This will allow us to install in a building specially built for us; the first part of the equipment for the international station, and will give us a range that will be adequate for all our needs."[1]

Today, Interpol's radio network effectively covers the planet. Working around the clock, operators at the International Bureau in Paris St. Cloud, send urgent messages vibrating through thousands of miles into remote corners of the earth.

The notion — frequently expressed by the organization's critics — that because the system still employs the old Morse code, it is inefficient — is not supported by the facts.

While it cannot be compared with the kind of high-speed, electronic data processing provided by the computer which Interpol now has in the planning stage, as a means for carrying on day-to-day police work, the system functions better than would appear at first sight.

One reason for this is the use of single code words to express an entire, standardized dispatch. By way of illustration: Mr. X, a suspected drug trafficker travelling on a Venezuelan passport, is detained by the Italian police. They ask the National Central Bureau in Rome to query Interpol 1B in Paris for the background, full identification, and criminal history, if any, of the person in custody.

The operator at Interpol headquarters can request all this information from Caracas NCB by flashing the single vocable "SOPEF" to the regional station at Buenos Aires for immediate relay to the Venezualan capital. In the Interpol Phrase Code (a system inherited from the Nazis), "SOPEF" means, "Please send all relevant information you may possess or be able to acquire about this person. Please include his photograph and fingerprints, details of any previous convictions and, if he is wanted, please inform us whether extradition is or will be requested and under what conditions."

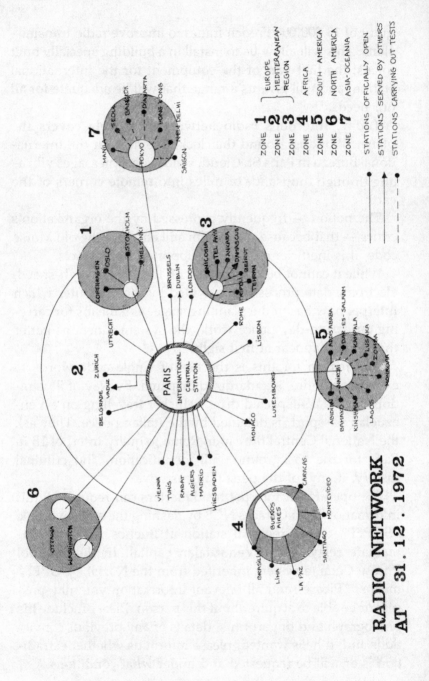

**RADIO NETWORK
AT 31.12.1972**

ZONE **1** EUROPE
ZONE **2** MEDITERRANEAN
ZONE **3** REGION
ZONE **4** AFRICA
ZONE **5** SOUTH AMERICA
ZONE **6** NORTH AMERICA
ZONE **7** ASIA-OCEANIA

STATIONS OFFICIALLY OPEN
STATIONS SERVED BY OTHERS
STATIONS CARRYING OUT TESTS

PARIS INTERNATIONAL CENTRAL STATION

Zone 1: COPENHAGEN, OSLO, STOCKHOLM, HELSINKI, BRUSSELS, DUBLIN, LONDON

Zone 2: UTRECHT, ZURICH, BELGRADE, VADUZ, MONACO, LUXEMBOURG, VIENNA, TUNIS, RABAT, ALGIERS, MADRID, WIESBADEN

Zone 3: PHILOSIA, TEL AVIV, ANKARA, DAMASCUS, BEIRUT, TEPRN, ROME, LISBON

Zone 4: BRASILIA, LIMA, LA PAZ, SANTIAGO, MONTEVIDEO, CARACAS, BUENOS AIRES

Zone 5: ADDIS ABABA, DAR-ES-SALAAM, KAMPALA, LUSAKA, ZOMBA, MONROVIA, LAGOS, KINSHASA, BAMAKO, ABIDJAN

Zone 6: OTTAWA, WASHINGTON

Zone 7: MANILA, SEOUL, BANGKOK, DJAKARTA, HONG KONG, NEW DELHI, SAIGON, TOKYO

In a priority request of this kind, it is usually only a matter of hours before the inquiring agency has a reply.

Global data sharing

The control room at the International Bureau is equipped with positions for six operators, who are linked by cable circuits to 16 powerful transmitters installed on a site at Lagnysur-Marne, some 40-odd miles south of Paris. In addition, the Central radio room at St. Cloud is furnished with 15 crystal-controlled, and three continuous band receivers. There is also a teletype machine connected to a radio teleprinter network into which are plugged those European bureaus which handle a large amount of traffic.

Rounding out Interpol's system of police business and information sharing on a global scale, are messages transmitted by telephone, cable, airmail and surface post.

The documents which deserve our closest attention are those known as "international descriptive circulations." These fall into four categories, each designated by a color tab in much the same way that Himmler arranged his files.

Black-tab circulations are simply queries concerning unidentified dead bodies. They may or may not involve criminal activities; usually they do not. A description of the deceased, together with any details about his or her death, if known, are included in the dispatch.

Top-priority circulations are indicated by a red corner. These are messages identifying and describing wanted persons who should be arrested when found, and held for extradition to the member-country originating the action.

Owing to the fact that the red-check dispatch constitutes what is known as a "seek, hold and deliver" order, Interpol urges member countries to use caution in requesting the international bureau to issue them. Three prerequisite conditions are cited, viz., that the offense alleged against the individual is a violation of common law; a warrant for his arrest is outstanding; or, the police agency requesting the arrest has the authority to apply for extradition when the wanted person is taken into custody.

Blue-tab circulations are requests for information about suspects. The latter are generally persons who are unknown to the International Bureau, or concerning whom they have but scanty details. They are persons whom some police authority has judged to be "unreliable." Each NCB receiving the circular is asked to provide as much background as possible about the individual, including his true name, aliases, present whereabouts, arrests, convictions, life-style, associates and so on. Innocent persons as well as criminals may have a file started on them in this way.

Green-tab circulations are intended to direct N.C.B.'s attention to a given individual, and to suggest that he ought to be watched, even though he is not wanted for any crime.

Very simply, the green-cornered bulletin is one way in which Interpol implements its theory of pre-delinquent action. "It is impossible," declared M. Nepote, IP Secretary General, "to determine beforehand whether or not someone may become involved in some form of criminal activity. This explains why the various institutions of the 122 countries which work together within the I.C.P.O. have full power to exchange information in comformity with the provisions of the Organizations Constitution."[2]

In effect, this procedure puts the finger on people who, under the Anglo-Saxon common law are legally innocent. It violates the individual's right to freedom of movement without constant police observation and, in some countries, harrassment. It also produces or adds to a secret dossier on the monitored individual at the international level. The NCB under whose initiative the police carry out the surveillance is requested to send full details concerning the suspect in question and to report his movements to Interpol Paris.

Very often the police who invigilate the suspect are unaware that they are, in fact, acting for Interpol. Jean-Jacques Marc, a senior Interpol official attached to the organization's world headquarters in Paris, explained it this way:

"Asked to check whether Mr. X did indeed stay at the beach hotel from 5th May to 9th January, the low-ranking detective in Pizagua (Chile) or the constable in Dunedin (New Zealand) is perhaps unaware that he is acting as a genuine 'Interpol agent.' "[3]

The quality and accuracy of the information sent back to the IP files by a "low-ranking detective" in Uganda or a secret police agent in Communist Roumania is a question that calls for transcendental meditation.

Lastly, there is once again the disturbing thought that the data collected in this way become part of a permanent record which at some future time may be circulated worldwide or leaked to private persons or groups who will misuse it.

Recognizing the dangers that lurk in the latter possibility, former Secretary General Marcel Sicot warned Interpol members:

"I must stress the fact that the consequences may be very serious should any person divulge information from international circulations to any persons whatever outside the police forces."[4]

These words must have returned to haunt the inner sanctum of the General Secretariat at St. Cloud in 1974, when the Church of Scientology filed legal suits in Germany, France, Great Britain and the United States, alleging that the church and its founder had been grossly libeled by material leaked from an Interpol dossier.

There is one fact (which often escapes notice) that must be taken into account when reviewing the procedures at Interpol's international bureau. It is the predominantly French character of the administrative staff. Currently, out of 160 employees at the St. Cloud headquarters, only about 20 are non-French. Of that number, one police officer and one translator are American.

Moreover, the Paris NCB is fully integrated into the French Police Nationale, being the 3rd Bureau of the Judicial Police. Nominally, the head of French Interpol is the director of the *Police Judiciaire* (the department for criminal investigations), but at present he has delegated his authority to the deputy director.

The French system

In view of this close alliance between Interpol and the French machinery of justice, it might be useful to examine the latter. Few non-French who have not resided in the Republic or been involved with the police of that country, realize how completely the French system differs from that of the other Western democracies.

To begin with, French police exercise broad powers that no other law-enforcement agency this side of the Iron Curtain can legally claim.

Functioning under a legal code that in large part goes back to the seventeenth century, the French police force "is bound by no rules and takes no heed of legal complications or the legal rights of the individual."

In his work, *The State of France*, Swiss historian Herbert Lüthy likewise reminds us that the prefect of police unites under his control, political administrative and judicial powers "like an absolute king within his realm." He can at any time, "at his own discretion and upon his own authority and responsibility, and in the absence of any charge or evidence that a crime has been committed, and without the sanction of any judicial authority, issue warrants, keep people under arrest for unlimited periods, conduct interrogations and inquiries, order houses to be searched, confiscate letters in the post, hand people over to the machinery of justice, release them or deliver them to a lunatic asylum."

One wonders what the people of France are celebrating so fervently on Bastille Day.

As Dr. Lüthy further observes, while human and civil rights are a French gift to the world, she forgot to bequeath to herself a habeas corpus Act, which is a cornerstone of the Anglo-Saxon system of justice.

The French policeman's insatiable curiosity and enthusiasm for surveillance is traditional. Balzac called him "suspicion incarnate."

Similarly, his penchant for collecting and filing derogatory information based upon gossip and rumour has always been a salient feature of his professional character. In fact, the French may be said to be the inventors of the secret dossier, dating back to the despotic days of Louis XIV.

"The existence of these dossiers remains unknown to those whom they concern, and they have no opportunity of correcting them, because they are never aware of their contents. But from the police point of view, it is always well to be ready for all eventualities and 'to have something at hand' against everyone."[5]

It is only fair to add that the Gallic system seems to work — *for the French*. Writing of Paris, Philip John Stead commented, "All the elements of the totalitarian state are present in the unlimited and impenetrable sway of this police system, and yet the atmosphere of the city over which they preside is the freest in the world." Stead then quotes a remark of Yves Guyot: " 'The citizen is free to do whatever he likes, but under police supervision.' "[6]

However, even if the French police have, over the centuries, found just the right balance between despotism and freedom (and there are recent signs that this equilibrium is being tilted toward the despotic) the system is no more exportable than a Bordeaux vineyard.

That is why Interpol's French connection will continue to be a matter of growing concern, especially when that instrument of dossier dictatorship — the computer — makes its appearance at St. Cloud.

Fears have been expressed in France as well as abroad, that Interpol's period of Nazi control, as well as its postwar term under the influence of former SS officers and collaborators may have left a permanent imprint on the organization.

As recently as February 13, 1976, a Paris daily — *Le Quotidien* — raised the question of whether the attitudes of Interpol's European staff had not been coloured by the organization's undesirable antecedents.

The article noted that on 12 March 1972, when a new agreement between Interpol and the French government had been signed, it was stated in that protocol that Interpol had ceased to exist during World War II. The paper then cited the documentary evidence, reviewed in previous pages of this work, proving the contrary.

A police-state mould

Even so, the article continued, the matter would be merely a fact of history if it were not that the police-state mould had persisted after the war owing to the presence of former pro-Nazis who occupied key positions in the organization. The paper referred to the case of Paul Dickopf as being of particular interest, since he was Interpol president from 1967 to 1972.

In spite of revelations concerning Interpol's wartime history and Herr Dickopf's own background, Secretary General Nepote has continued to rationalize both. His argument runs like this:

It is wrong to reproach the present-day Interpol for what

happened in the war years. The transfer of the IP headquarters from Vienna to Berlin, and the organization's operation by the Nazis were carried out without the consent of the General Assembly.

"At this time, the Germans said to themselves, the chief of the German police is the president of Interpol. And I should say, they had some historical background for that. Between the two world wars, Interpol was a very small organization. It was strongly linked with the Austrian police, because it had no funds and so on. And it was at this time a tradition which had been included in the regulations — I think orginally out of respect for the founder of the organization, Mr. Schober, who was Chief of Police of Austria — that the president of Interpol would be chief of police of the host country. So when the Nazis took Austria, and without any designation at the international level, they said Austria equals Germany, so the chief of police of Germany will be the president of Interpol."

This admission that the Nazis had acted in accordance with Interpol regulations when they appointed Reinhard Heydrich president of the association, contravened an earlier statement by M. Nepote in which he said the Nazi take-over had been illegal and compared it to a bank robbery.

In any case, he added, "during the war, the political police of Germany had their own files and their own agents, so they did not need Interpol at all. They had their own system much better than the Interpol machinery."[7]

The Secretary General side-stepped the fact that the Interpol files became a part of that machinery. Notices of arrest warrants were circulated via the Interpol publication. In cases where the wanted person was a Jew, the bulletin identified him as "Jewish type," "Mosaic," or simply, "Jew."

The crimes for which these fugitives were wanted tell their own tragic story: falsification of baptismal certificates, travelling papers, etc., to be used in escaping Nazi persecution.

During the same interview in which he made this state-

ment, M. Nepote later said that before U.S. authorities returned the IP files following Germany's surrender ("They
came from Berlin by the American Air Lift"), they were
purged and checked, and that Interpol also spent five or six
years sifting them for Nazi input. "And we found some good,
some interesting documents."

As for Paul Dickopf, the former SS officer who was part of
the "hierarchy of terror" known as the Sicherheitsdienst (S.
D.) and more recently president of Interpol, M. Nepote offered that thread-bare pleading that has been the stock-in-
trade of almost every former cog in Himmler's huge
murder-machine: he acted under duress and because his only
alternative was the concentration camp or the firing squad.

M. Nepote, who was a close friend of the postwar, de-
Nazified Herr Dickopf explained:

"When the German army was mobilized, you see, they
called all men into the army. Dickopf, a German citizen, was
called up and he received an assimilated rank in the SS, which
was not the Gestapo. You know, it was quite different. The SS
was more or less the Sicherheit Security Service, or something
like that. And he was appointed to the counter-espoinage in
Stuttgart, the city where he was working.

"I have seen some documents saying he was in the SS
school or something like this. Possibly, I don't know. But I'm
not astonished because they did not ask him if he would like
to go or not, because you see, he was in the machine. The
American soldiers during the war were not asked if they
would agree to fight in Okinawa. They were sent there and
they had to fight. You agree on that, eh! He was mobilized.
The same system exists, I'm sure, in the British army.

"This was the case of Dickopf. When he realized what was
happening in Germany with the political system, he deserted
his post and lived for one year in Brussels, hidden by a family
he knew, and I know, because he told me personally many
times.

"After one year — I mean in September '43 — he walked by night from Brussels to the Swiss border, because I go sometimes by car, and I know the place where he crossed the border. It was night between one and two o'clock, I think in June '43, he crossed the border and told the Swiss, 'I am a deserter from the German army and I ask political status as a refugee." This status was given to him and he stayed in Switzerland until 1947."

A cozening apology

The reader has only to refer to the documented facts concerning Dickopf's Nazi years, given in Chapter 4, to appreciate the cozening simplicity of this apologia. Yet it was made by a European police officer of forty-odd years' experience, the past twelve of which he has been the administrative head of Interpol.

It would appear that the illogic of Dickopf's taking refuge in Belgium, which had fallen to the Germans two years previously and was under tight Nazi control, especially when Switzerland was only an hours drive from Karlsruhe, where he was stationed, never crossed M. Nepote's mind. It seems fair to ask: Why did Dickopf choose to spend a year under the Gestapo's nose in Brussels before seeking asylum in Switzerland? This meant that he had to cross Europe two times, allegedly as a fugitive and an important one at that, being an officer of the elite SS.

Although Dickopf is said to have deserted the SS in 1942, a notation on the official records of the Security Office indicates that no warrant was issued for his arrest until October 1944 — two years after he defected. Skeptics point out that this was only six months before the fall of Berlin. At that time, Himmler and his top aides were making renewed peace feelers to the

West. Many of these overtures were directed to Allen Dulles, head of the OSS, a forerunner of the CIA, and "the most influential White House man in Europe," whose headquarters was in Berne, Switzerland.

Dulles, who once said he would work "with the Devil himself" to aid the Allied war effort, met secretly with a number of Himmler's agents who had been sent to talk things over.

There was no actual arrest warrant in Dickopf's file — merely the notation that one had been issued.

Researchers, however, have found no record of a warrant in the files of the Gestapo, criminal police, or army during that period. There is no record of a court-martial in absentia and no record of his wartime service, except for brief notices of promotion and postings.

The latter circumstance could be accounted for by the fact that Dickopf was an intelligence officer; files of secret agents, with their detailed service records, were locked away elsewhere. They were inaccessible to all save senior officers of the S.D.

When asked concerning Dickopf's activities after he entered Switzerland, M. Nepote said the former SS officer never discussed that part of his career, and the Interpol chief did not press him concerning it. "I must say, I was always very discreet.

"I know he was in residence in Chevenez in a small hotel, but I don't know what he did, you see, exactly."

Various accounts, some emanating from Dickopf himself, have been circulated concerning his sojourn in Switzerland as a wartime internee.

One officially approved version is that he pursued studies in criminology at the University of Berne and the University of Lausanne. However, neither of these institutions have a record of his enrollment either as a full-time student or as a regular "listener" (that is, a person attending lectures without sitting for examinations or credit).

Prof. Mathier, head of the Institute of Police Science and Criminology at the University of Lausanne was certain that Dickopf had not studied at the Institute, even though he had heard it said that Dickopf had claimed he had done so.

Prof. Mathier said that his predecessor at the Institute, Dr. Bischoff, had told him that Dickopf had stayed for some time on a farm near a village called St. Saphorin sur Morges, about 15 kilometers west of Lausanne.

Most doubts and difficulties about Dickopf's Swiss experience could be resolved if one could see inside his File (No. N12673), kept by the Eidgenössische Fremdenpolizei (Swiss Foreigners' Police) in Berne. But that dossier is apparently under protective seal against the dissecting examination of journalists. An official at the department intimated with almost telepathic subtlety, that the contents of Herr Dickopf's thick file might not fully support the story that he was an anti-Nazi Nazi.

Dickopf and the OSS

One chapter of the Dickopf saga, at least, is sustained by available documentation. That is the part which tells of his serving the American OSS in Switzerland: "While in Switzerland, Paul Dickopf contacted the American authorities, informed them of his situation well before the end of World War II, and cooperated with them."[8]

An East German publication states the same thing in somewhat different terms: "He became, like thousands of other collaborators — of the Gehlen Service, SD abroad, SD internal and other criminal police organizations after 1945 — an agent of the American secret service and functioned later as an advisor on criminal police questions for the U.S. Military

Government, which put him in 1950 at the disposal of the Bonn Ministry of Interior as an expert."

The copy of a letter which came into my possession, as well as Dickopf's postwar career, indicate that both these statements are correct. It is written on the stationery of the American Legation in Berne, Switzerland and is dated September 6, 1945. It reads:

"To Whom It May Concern:

"Mr. Paul Dickopf, a German National, has been a political refugee since 1942. He fled to Switzerland in July 1943, was interned and only late in 1944 was free to give me his wholehearted cooperation.

"Since that time Mr. Dickopf has been of very great service to me. His wide knowledge of German organization and personalities has been invaluable; he is a trained member of the Kriminalpolizei and I have drawn extensively upon his experience for information on War Crimes and Criminals.

"Mr. Dickopf has made many friends among Swiss Police officials and these contacts also have been most useful. In the confused period that followed the German capitulation, when Switzerland was deciding what was to be done with the German nationals within her borders, Mr. Dickopf was my intermediary with the authorities on a number of occasions and gave me repeated proof of his tact and discretion.

"He is a man of intelligence, of superior education and, above all, of exceptional personal integrity. I regret to see him leave Switzerland and I warmly recommend him to the Allied authorities in his homeland, to which he now returns.

Paul C. Blum"

It will be noted that Paul C. Blum, who signed the foregoing letter, gave himself no identifying rank or title. He was, in fact, a trusted agent of Allen Dulles, who at that time was in charge of the OSS operation in Switzerland.

Born in Yokohama, Japan, Blum was a naturalized American citizen and a graduate of Yale University, where he took a degree in philosophy.

Although a specialist in Far Eastern affairs, he was employed by the U.S. State Department as Economic Attaché at Lisbon in October 1944, when he received his assignment to the OSS in Berne to do counter-espionage work. As a cover for his intelligence activities, he was given the designation of Clerk at the American Legation.

It was with considerable difficulty that I traced and finally located Mr. Blum, who is presently a resident of Tokyo, although he was in New York during our exchange.

A former member of the OSS team in Switzerland had described Blum as "a very reticent man," and predicted that unless he had changed considerably in the intervening years, I would find him reluctant to provide details of his work in wartime intelligence.

My informant's forecast proved to be quite accurate. Blum said merely that the information I had received concerning Dickopf "is certainly at variance with the facts as I knew them at the time in Switzerland. I had good reason then, as I do now, to believe in his bona fides."

He would not reveal, however, just what that "good reason" was based upon. When I disclosed some of the documented evidence which clearly proves that Dickopf was not a conscripted Nazi with an "assimilated" SS rank, his response echoed almost verbatim the sweet reasonableness of the statement made by M. Nepote:

"The facts you give regarding Paul Dickopf," said Blum, "while unfamiliar, in no way surprise me. In those early, heady days of the Hitler régime any German bureaucrat who sought advancement must have found it politic, if not necessary, to join the Nazi party. Able and ambitious young police officer that he was. Dickopf must have been well aware that he had little choice. Knowing him, I can see how, later, he would find his position untenable, his assignments unacceptable. Whether his flight to Switzerland was real or feigned is not the point, it seems to me; it got him out of Germany and the party. Once there, he behaved extremely well. The Swiss saw to that, you may be sure, and they as well as we, were thoroughly satisfied that he did not betray the trust we reposed in him."

That is all very well, but the question remains: what does Mr. Blum know about Dickopf that we don't know, and that he does not care to tell?

The OSS, like its successor the CIA, never let unimportant things like ideology stand in the way of recruiting a good agent. And those who carried out their mission successfully were rewarded with the agency's loyal support.

Back in the saddle

In Dickopf's case that meant acceptance by the Allied Military Government. It meant also that he had influential backing in establishing himself once more in Germany's law-inforcement machinery. He was one of the first former police officers to be called to work in the Federal Republic's reorganized Ministry of the Interior where, during the ensuing three years he laid the foundations for the Bundeskriminalamt (the federal criminal police) headquartered at Wiesbaden.

As M. Nepote tells it:

"He spoke French very well. And as he had no Nazi background [sic] he was sent as a member of the first German delegation which came back into Interpol in 1952. He attended all the Interpol meetings after that. He was a very clever man, very quiet and I should say, democratic. He was very popular among the Interpol general assembly, so he was elected President by secret ballot. Everybody knew him be-

Jean Nepote, present secretary-general of Interpol, who directs the global activities of the police organization.

cause he had been in the organization for 20 years. I never heard one word from anyone about his background."[9]

On the face of it, M. Nepote's own background would seem to be impeccable. The son of a miner and factory worker, he was born in 1915 in Normandy. After attending the secondary school in Rouen, he worked his way through the University of Lyon, where he earned a law degree. After graduation, he joined the French police as a clerk at the Prefecture of Rhone, but the following year was called into the army, mobilized to defend his country against invasion.

After the French army collapsed before the overwhelming onslaught of the German blitzkrieg, Nepote returned briefly to his job at the Rhone Prefecture, but said that he did not like the work there, which he considered the job of a civil servant.

He requested and, in April 1941, was granted a year's leave without pay. He was not, however, cutting himself adrift during a parlous period of his country's history. According to a decision by the Ministry of Interior, dated 13 March 1941, Jean Nepote had been appointed to the Sureté Nationale (the national security police) as a superintendent in training in the Director General's office. He was assigned to the central files section. These were the general archives of the police, and the duties of that department were defined in the Bulletin Officiel of the Interior Ministry as "the managing and keeping up-to-date of the files relating to the general police and the judicial police; the setting up of dossiers; the printing and dissemination of files covering investigations of individuals who were the subjects of justice warrants, expelled foreigners; absentees, deserters, illegal sojourn in the country; and debtors who owed the Treasury."

Nepote has said that during the war years, he worked with a unit of the French Resistance known by the code name, Ajax. It is, in fact, a matter of record that he received a decoration from General De Gualle for his assistance to the underground freedom fighters during that period. He is also a

Chevalier of the Legion of Honour.

In spite of this impressive curriculum vitae, M. Nepote's attachment to the national police at a time when that force was under control of the Nazis has made him suspect in the eyes of some observers, both in France and abroad.

Pointing out that Himmler had ordered Heydrich to install a *Sonderkommando* (autonomous command with a special mission) at the same time Paris fell to German troops on 14 June 1490 — almost a year before Nepote joined the Sureté, — one critic said:

"Jean Nepote voluntarily joined what could be called the French department of the Nazi German police force."

Critics insist that the Director General's office to which M. Nepote was assigned was in Paris and under Nazi control.

They note that the French national police of 1941 included such units as those dealing with "internment camps," "liquidation," "those returning to nations occupied by the Reich," and "anti-semitism."

It is recalled that under the law of October 4, 1940, stateless Jews were subject to internment. The German Jews who had fled to unoccupied France were promptly interned at a camp in Gurs where one report says they "lived in crowded barracks, sleeping on the ground, devoured by vermin, suffering from hunger and cold in a damp muddy region."

Raul Hilberg writes that by 1941 the Vichy government had established in Southern France a network of camps at Gurs, Rivesaltes, Noé, Récébédon, La Vernet, and Les Milles.

In Paris, under the direction of an SS "Jewish expert," the Paris prefecture of police compiled a card index in which every Jew was listed alphabetically, together with his street address, profession, and nationality.

Allegations of this kind greatly anger M. Nepote. He declared recently, "It has been said on Dutch television by somebody that Monsieur Nepote was a collaborator, that he was appointed in Paris at his request during the war." Then, striking his desk for emphasis, he added: "I never put one foot in Paris during the war. I stayed in the free zone of France."

It is quite conceivable that the Interpol General Secretary did, as he maintains, provide valuable assistance to the French underground in his job at the Sureté headquarters. What is less understandable is that, as a former member of the French resistance movement, he could be the staunch apologist of an ex-SS officer like Dickopf or the close friend of collaborators and sublimated Nazis who held key positions in Interpol after its revival in 1946.

Documents unearthed during research for this book reveal that one French Police Commissaire still on the staff of Interpol's international bureau, served under the Vichy government during the Nazi occupation of France. A notice in the *Journal Officiel* of 18 September 1942 states that he was appointed police inspector in training by the Ministry of Interior.

After the war, he was suspended from his police duties when the liberators of France under De Gualle conducted a purge of collaborators and undersirable elements in the administration.

At some subsequent date, however, he was reinstated in the French police system and today holds an important post in Interpol's St. Cloud headquarters.

Whatever connection some of Interpol's key personnel may or may not have had with that organization's wartime operations, one Nazi practice has been rigorously preserved. That is the creation and maintenance of secret files, sealed against outside inspection. And secret they are, despite official denials from St. Cloud. Not only are they secret, but in some cases, IP officials deny that they exist.

Once again, a case in point is that of the Church of Scientology. When David Gaiman, director of public affairs for the church, first approached Interpol officials at that organization's international bureau, he was informed that Interpol did not have a file on Scientology or its founder. They cited Article

III in Interpol's constitution, which proscribes any intervention or activities by the organization of a political, military, religious, or racial character.

Like all such denials by official file-keepers, the Interpol disclaimer was false.

On the 26th of March 1975, Gaiman journeyed to Paris for a face-to-face meeting with M. Nepote. He took with him documents proving that information had been circulated by Interpol's National Central Bureaux containing falsehoods.

The Secretary General said he would ask the appropriate national authorities to check the authenticity of the documents and, if their reports confirmed that items of information disseminated in the past did, in fact, contain errors, he would take the necessary steps to have them corrected.

Less than a month later, Gaiman found it necessary to write M. Nepote, drawing his attention to the fact that in spite of the understanding reached during their meeting at St. Cloud, (that no further information on the church would be disseminated until the various NCBs had checked the documents correcting the file) the Social Styrelsen in Sweden had been given the defamatory Weisbaden report. Under Swedish law, this document was on open file, available to the press and the public. The repute of the church in Sweden had already been damaged by it.

Gaiman added that he had also learned that an Inspector Marshall of the Canadian Interpol office had told a church representative in that country that he, too, had received the report and that an investigation of the church at the local police level was being conducted in Canadian cities.

"How many such investigations are in progress, I know not," the letter read. "One thing is certain, however, and that is that the first grounds for suspicion seem to have emanated from the Interpol report."

In reply, M. Nepote denied that the General Secretariat had given any information concerning the Church of Scientology to any person whatsoever since their March 26 meeting. As for other Interpol bureaux, said M. Nepote, they were autonomous and free to follow any course they saw fit.

Insult to injury

A short time later, the church's world headquarters staff in England learned that Interpol had passed documents containing some of the false data to a French official named Andreani at the Palais de Justice. Gaiman asked Nepote for some explanation of this action in view of their previous understanding.

No explanation was forthcoming. Instead, in a three-line letter, one of M. Nepote's deputies responded for him, "I have absolutely no information enabling me to answer your enquiry."

Meanwhile, the church's efforts in the U.S. had shown slightly better results. James B. Clawson, deputy assistant secretary for operations at the U.S. Treasury Department informed the Church that their corrective documents would be added to the existing file in Interpol's Washington bureau, and would be included with any future circulations. Also, the amending data provided by the Church would be sent to recipients of the prior material.

Unlike certain of his colleagues, Clawson from the outset seemed genuinely interested in striking a balance between what he regarded as the legitimate need of government for information and the individual's or group's right to inspect and, where necessary to correct, that file.

The U.S. Department of Labour, one of whose functionaries, — named Foley — had propagated a calumnious report on the Church, also agreed to set the record straight. Craig A. Berrington, the department's associate solicitor for manpower said he had advised the Employment and Training Administration to whom the report had first been sent, that the Foley memorandum was "irrelevant, unverified and based on hearsay" and that the document should be destroyed.

With these two victories to cheer him on, David Gaiman once more turned his attention to the uncorrected dossier at Interpol's international bureau. Continuing to press M. Nepote for a satisfactory response to the Scientologists' demands that the file be purged, Gaiman also urged that Interpol adhere to the provisions of its charter which prohibit intervention in matters that involve religion.

Referring to Nepote's argument that the 122 countries that work together in Interpol have full power to exchange information, because it is impossible to determine in advance whether someone may become involved in some form of criminal activity, Gaiman told the General Secretary:

"If one follows the logical sequence deriving from your point, every citizen of every country holding membership in Interpol is potentially the subject of a dossier. I am horrified at the prospect, since it validates an American correspondent's view that 'Interpol is a kingdom of police over which no sovereign nation has any power of control.' "

Eventually, on 17 February 1976, M. Nepote wrote Gaiman a final letter informing him that Interpol Washington, which had been kept informed of the points raised during the course of their discussions had received documentation from the Church of Scientology in the U.S. and had been sent by the U.S. authorities to all countries concerned and to Interpol St. Cloud. "Consequently, all the authorities concerned have now been given the necessary clarifications."

Did this mean that the false record had been corrected, or merely that something had been added, namely, the documentation which the Church claimed to be proof of previous error?

After all the research, discussions, protests, legal records, meetings and correspondence, would the permanent central file at Interpol IB remain as it was?

Well, as the French say, *"Plus ça change, plus c'est la même chose:* The more it changes, the more it's the same thing."

> *"Insinuations are the rhetoric of the Devil."*
>
> — Goethe

12. *The Devil's Rhetoric*

One of the more insidious aspects of secret dossier keeping is its use for circulating *false* information.

This activity, known to intelligence services as disinformation diffusion, is an outgrowth of a wartime practice employed to deceive and mislead the enemy. It should not, however, be confused with black propaganda, another maneuvre to which it is closely related. The difference between the two stratagems is this:

Disinformation depends for its success upon the secrecy with which the fake or ambiguous data are disseminated. It is most effective when it can pass through confidential channels to various terminals (such as law-enforcement agencies) where it will be accepted as fact and acted upon because it emanated from an official source. So long as the spurious report remains unknown to anyone outside the closed circuit, its effectiveness is unimpaired. There is small likelihood of someone knowledgeable coming across it and challenging its accuracy.

Black propaganda, per contra, is the technique of the Big Lie, publicly proclaimed, widely distributed and as frequently repeated as possible.

During the Hitler era in Germany, the Nazis used both black propaganda and disinformation. In their campaign against the Jews, Dr. Goebbels force-fed the media a steady diet of provocative stories about the "Jewish plot," etc. At the same time, non-Jewish opposition to the régime was removed from positions of power by means of disinformation planted in secret files and circulated by governmental agencies, especially the police.

In our present age of duplicity, disinformation has come to be a prime tool of international espionage services, like those of the CIA, KGB, MI6 and so on; and of law-enforcement agencies on all levels.

In his chilling exposé of the Russian KGB, John Barron says that *Disinformatsiya* (Department A), has emerged as one of the most important sections of the Soviet espionage apparatus. The operation's principal aim is the global poisoning of public opinion. It includes clandestine schemes "to compromise and undermine the prestige of individuals active in U.S. politics and government," (who are hostile to the Soviet Union); influence the decisions of foreign powers; and to generally demoralize Western societies.

As countless instances bear witness, all police file-keepers, whether the FBI, Interpol or the precinct station around the corner, are not as interested in the accuracy of their records as in their utility. If half-truths, malicious lies or mistaken charges appear likely to serve their purpose, even at some future time, they are retained, even when documented evidence calls for their correction.

Prof. H. Taylor Buckner, a Canadian researcher who made a study of the subject, reported recently that police exist outside the rest of society and rely upon deceit and secrecy to do their job. He said duplicity is taught as part of their formal instruction, and through the police manual.

Prof. Buckner found that officers use deception to control situations in which they have no legal authority to act, "sometimes including uncovering information, controlling distressing but legal behaviour, gaining the right to search, justifying some arrests, or getting a confession. The practice of lying in many different situations becomes absolutely normal for them."[1]

An interesting feature of the Scientology case against Interpol is that the disinformation contained in the Church's dossier was, owing to a leak, used as black propaganda. As their German counsel notes in his legal brief:

"First of all, the victims came to know of the existence of the disinformation. Only suspected hitherto, as a cause of their troubles, its actuality was confirmed and thus an opportunity to sue and to correct the false information arose.

"Secondly, the sources and principal carriers of the disinformation became known to the intended victims, and were exposed to view, so the entire mechanism backfired along the route whence it originated."

The chain of events in Germany which led up to the legal action against Interpol, began in August 1972. On that date, the German Church of Scientology published an article in their newspaper *Freiheit*, attacking the Max Planck Institute of Psychiatry in Munich for alleged abuses in its treatment of mental patients.

The publication recalled the unpleasant fact that the Max

Planck Institute had formerly been the Kaiser Wilhelm Institute for Brain Research during the Nazi era. It quoted testimony from the Nuremburg trials of war criminals, which revealed German psychiatry's direct involvement in shocking atrocities, including the so-called Euthanasia Murders.

The Church had an abundance of documented horror stories to choose from. Postwar reports of investigations carried out by medical and scientific teams tell of crimes so monstrous that even in our day of violence and brutality, they push the mind to the edge of madness.

In his important, but terrifying work, *A Sign For Cain*, Dr. Frederic Wertham has compellingly drawn attention to the fact that it was not a handful of sadistic Nazi butchers who carried out the mass destruction of mental patients; it was the psychiatric profession as a whole.

"Life devoid of value"

Furthermore, the idea of killing "worthless human beings" was not a Nazi invention, as commonly believed. The concept derives from an influential book called *The Destruction of Life Without Value*, published in Leipzig in 1920. It was co-authored by Dr. Alfred Hoche, psychiatrist; and Karl Binding, an eminent jurist.

The authors speak of those who are below the level of beasts and argue that they represent a foreign body in human society "whose death is urgently necessary." Dr. Hoche decries any feeling of sympathy for these unfortunate beings, declaring that such an emotion is based on "erroneous thinking."

Dr. Wertham says the book influenced — or crystallized — the thinking of a whole generation. Almost without exception, leading psychiatrists in Germany (and elsewhere) embraced the notion that they were competent to pronounce value judgments not only on individuals on medical grounds, but on whole groups, on medico-sociological grounds.

It began as a rationalization of "mercy killings," and help for the suffering, the incurable, the dying (the same arguments that are starting to appear again in the current literature). It then progressed to wider and wider criteria, taking in "psychopathic personalities, epileptics, encephalitics, neurological cases, mental defectives of both severe and mild degree, arteriosclerotics, deaf-mutes, patients with all kinds of nervous diseases, handicapped patients who had lost a limb in the first World War and were in a state hospital, 'cripples' of every description, et al."[2]

Finally, it was generalized in the term "useless eaters," which included the aged, the infirm, the misfits, the undesirables, the unproductive. In a word, it meant extermination of the weak.

To conceal its purpose and extent, the whole project was given the euphemistic designation, Euthanasia Action. It has been described as "a model of the most bureaucratic mass murder in history." As Dr. Wertham reminds us, the wholesale killings had nothing whatever to do with euthanasia (a Greek word meaning "good death"). "They were not mercy deaths, but merciless murders. . . . These victims were not dying, they were not in pain, they were not suffering, and most of them were not incurable."

Moreover, they suffered horrible death-agonies by gassing, lethal injections, starvation, and experimental medical procedures. Before the gas chambers were dismantled and moved eastward to the concentration camps, the psychiatrists had put to death an estimated 275,000 "patients" in their killing centers at Sonnestein, Berlin-Buch, Kaufbeuren, Grafeneck and Hadamar.

At the latter institution, the full staff of psychiatrists, nurses, attendants and secretaries gathered in 1941 for a special ceremony to celebrate the cremation of the ten thousandth mental patient. Everybody received a free bottle of beer to commemorate the occasion.

Among the victims of the "life devoid of value" operation were thousands of children and infants. A special agency was set up to deal with them. The most prominent member of that commission, who decided which children would be killed was Dr. Werner Catel. It will probably take most readers unaware to learn that until a few years ago, Dr. Catel was professor of pediatrics at the University of Kiel. Still an advocate of child "euthanasia," he published a book in 1962 entitled, *Borderline Situations of Life* in which he defends the practice.

Spoon-fed death

The method most commonly employed for killing the children was incremental doses of Luminal, or other lethal drugs spoon-fed as medicine or mixed with their food. At the Eglfing-Haar state hospital, the victims were progressively starved to death. Dr. Pfannmueller, head of the institution, told one visitor that his method was "much simpler and more natural."

"With these words, the fat and smiling doctor lifted an emaciated, whimpering child from his little bed, holding him up like a dead rabbit. He went on to explain that food is not withdrawn all at once, but the rations are gradually decreased. 'With this child,' he added, 'it will take another two or three days.' "[3]

When this monster was finally brought to trial after the war, he was charged specifically with the murder of 120 children, and was sentenced to six years imprisonment, but was freed after serving only two. As Dr. Wertham observes, that makes about six days for each child that was killed.

It is salutary to bear in mind that the designers and directors of the entire assembly-line murder apparatus were the leading psychiatrists of pre-war Germany. A list of their names reads like a *Who's Who* of their profession. Among them were twelve full professors who held chairs in Germany's most prestigious universities. They are still quoted as authorities in present-day psychiatric texts. Even more important, many of their theories are still being taught and advocated — perhaps implemented — in today's practice of psychiatry.

Dr. Max de Crinis, professor of psychiatry at the University of Berlin, who played a leading role in the "euthanasia" murders, is eulogized in a recent psychiatric work as "a courageous and energetic physician." The book, which was highly recommended in an American journal of psychiatry, is entitled *Euthanasia and Destruction of Life Devoid of Value* (repeating almost verbatim, it should be remarked, the title of Dr. Alfred Hoche's work that, back in 1920, set the pattern for the mass extermination of "worthless lives"). The author, who is still professor of forensic and social psychiatry at the University of Marburg, barely alludes to "the comparatively few mental patients" killed in his preceptor's euthanasia programme.

Dr. Friedrich Manz, professor of psychiatry at the University of Münster since 1953, has said that his invitation to the euthanasia conference in Berlin, at which the monstrous project was planned, was "harmlessly formulated." Dr. Manz was one of the architects and founders of the World Federation For Mental Health, which today has affiliated national associations in every major country. These groups constitute formidable lobbies, influencing the legislation of all Western governments.

In tracing psychiatry's unbroken apostolic succession, it was learned that Dr. Julius Hallervorden, the notorious collector of human brains, was still a scientific member of the Max Planck Institute as late as 1957, when the organization's bulletin, *Metteilungen*, noted that he was observing his 75th birthday that year. The item also recalled that the German Federal Republic had honored Dr. Hallervorden with the Great Cross of Merit of the Order of Merit.

During the time the euthanasia programme was being carried out, Dr. Hallervorden was director of the pathology department at the Kaiser Wilhelm cerebral research center in Dillenberg. Eager to add to his already impressive collection of human brains, he asked his colleagues at the death establishments to send him the brains of the patients they murdered. As he told Major Leo Alexander of the British Army, who interrogated him afterward:

"I had heard that they were going to do that, that is to say, to kill some men in different establishments by means of carbon monoxide.

"I went to them and I said, 'Listen my friends', if you are going to kill all those people there, at least keep the brains so that we can use them.' They asked me, 'How many can you examine?' 'An unlimited number, the more the better,' I told them. I gave them clips, jars, boxes and the necessary instructions for removing and fixing the brain."[4]

In all, Dr. Hallervorden's confreres sent him 500 brains. "They came bringing them in like the delivery van from the furniture company," he said. They were dispatched in shipments of 150 to 200 at a time.

Researchers also discovered that Dr. Detlev Ploog, the present head of the Max Planck Institute, was formerly an associate of Dr. Helmut E. Ehrhardt, director of the Institute for Forensic and Social Psychiatry at the University of Marburg. Both worked under Dr. Werner Villinger who, until his suicide during preparations for the euthanasia trial at Limburg in 1961, was director of the University of Marburg Nervklinik.

Medal of honour

When the war ended, Dr. Villinger had continued his work and research in psychiatry and was decorated for "service and order" by the West German government. In 1950, he participated in the White House Conference on Children and Youth. Even after it was discovered that he had taken an active and decisive part in the euthanasia murders, his colleagues and admirers continued to defend his name.

In a glowing tribute to him, written after his death, Dr. Ehrhardt praises him as "a person deeply rooted in the Christian-humanistic tradition, an excellent teacher of youth, an always helpful and lovable colleague." He concludes by saying, "He will remain an ideal for us."

Dr. Ehrhardt is a fellow of the American Psychiatric Association and an executive board member of the World Federation For Mental Health. He co-edited (with Dr. Detlev Ploog) a memorial collection of Dr. Villinger's works, under the title, *Psychiatrie und Gesellschaft.*

The published attacks by the Church of Scientology proved extremely embarrassing to the Max Planck Institute. As a counter-measure, top officials of that organization asked the German authorities to obtain through police channels confidential information of a derogatory kind, which could be used to silence the critics.

The reader will recall that the eventual result of this machination, as described earlier in these pages, was to create more publicity than it was intended to suppress.

To recapitulate: the Federal Criminal Office (BKA) at Weisbaden responded to the Max Planck Institute's request for sensitive material on the Church of Scientology by asking the German bureau of Interpol to provide it. The latter had in its file a report, which had been written by two Scotland Yard officers named Price and Fyall, on the basis of a circulation sent to them by the FBI during that Bureau's dirty tricks" period.

Interpol London had passed the defamatory FBI-cum-Scotland Yard document to the German NCB in 1969. It was now made available to the BKA, where it was rewritten by two German policemen named Berk and Moschall. On March 8,

1973, it was released over the signature of Dr. Horst Herold, successor to Paul Dickopf as president of the Bundeskriminalamt.

The report was eventually circulated through official channels to 11 police stations, the Better Business Bureau and, of course, to the Max Planck Institute.

The latter leaked it to the press with the result that it spread quickly throughout the media, not only in Germany, but in Scandinavia and Holland as well. Herr Koenig, head of the Ministry of Interior, which has responsibility for the Criminal Office, admitted later that he knew the report was not being used in a criminal case, but to help the Max Planck Institute (a private association) to defend itself against the Scientologists.

The Federal Criminal Office likewise admitted in subsequent pleadings before the Weisbaden regional court that the report had been compiled deliberately "in order to protect the reputation of German psychiatry."

German tradition

To understand the experience of the Church in their attempts to seek redress in the courts, it is necessary to consider the history and background of German political tradition.

As Dr. Alan Westin once observed, the usages of democratic self-government came late to the Federal Republic. Authoritarian patterns are deeply rooted in the German social life, where there exists great respect — almost veneration — for officialdom and prestige. The result is that privileged elements, having the authority of family, wealth or official position, often enjoy rights denied the critic and non-conformist.

Some of the findings of the German courts in the Scientology case clearly reflect that inveteracy. By way of example:

Even though Dr. Horst Herald of the BKA had no legal right to pass on data from the Criminal Office's confidential files, the competent court held that Dr. Herold could not be made liable for his action because he had acted as an officer of the German state.

To discourage the Church from proceeding with their proposed litigation against Interpol, BKA, Dr. Herold, et al., the regional court at Weisbaden required the plaintiffs to pay extremely high security costs.

In one proceeding, brought before the court on November 13, 1974, the judge did not consider it necessary to hear any witnesses in order to reach a just decision.

The court found that the authoritative source of the Interpol report made it unnecessary for the defendants to question the truth or accuracy of its contents.

Of even greater significance in the present context, was the court's opinion that Interpol in Germany could not be sued because it did not have "the necessary prerequisites," that is, it was not a legal entity.

"In this ruling," declared Dr. Hans Kessler, the Church's legal counsel, "the court has expressed the opinion that an international organization which has — because of its membership — unlimited possibilities of influencing public affairs, and interfering directly in the private sphere of each German citizen, does not have to account for their acts."

"The only reason brought forward so far by the Federal Republic of Germany [for refusing to purge their files]," said Dr. Kessler, "is that the total state machinery would collapse if each citizen about whom false reports are contained in the files, wanted to correct them.

"Such an idea clearly shows how blindly German officialdom trusts 'authoritative' information, and how far from their proper official functions such false data have led them. They have gone so far afield, in fact, that they have violated their own regulations to make an innocent church the target of unjustified attacks.

"Neither Dr. Herold nor any of the other participants is

willing to promise not to further disseminate the report. Nobody is willing to withdraw the document nor initiate steps to amend it or repair the damage it has caused."

At this writing the church is pressing its legal fight in West Germany. Defendants include the Federal Criminal Office and its president; the Minister of the Interior; the Max Planck Institute and its director; Herbert Jeschke, head of German Interpol; the magazine *Neue Revue* (which first published the report) its editor, and publisher; and others.

Suits are also being filed in Sweden, Denmark, Holland, United Kingdom and Canada.

These actions will serve to clarify the legal aspects of official spying and file-keeping on an international scale, and for that we are all greatly in the Scientologists' debt.

As for prospects of a satisfactory outcome to their petitions asking correction of false dossiers, as well as irresponsible dissemination of their contents, only long-shot punters would seriously place a wager on that issue.

> "The danger of the past was that men became slaves. The danger of the future is that men may become robots."
>
> — Erich Fromm

13. Summary and Implications

In conclusion, let us summarize the facts concerning Interpol, as they have emerged during the investigation pursued in this study.

Interpol is, in a legal sense, a private, non-governmental organization, having never been established by international treaty among the countries represented in its membership.

It is covert, it is autonomous, it has an unsavoury history. Its two principal functions — the secret dossier system and pre-delinquent surveillance — are inquisitorial, therefore foreign to the Anglo-Saxon concept of liberty.

Of its 122 member states, the great majority — 85% — are non-democratic regimes embracing various political persuasions, many of which are in direct conflict with each other. A large number of these countries have political police patterned after the Nazi Gestapo or the Soviet KGB. People are arrested on suspicion and without warrant, held without trial, beaten or tortured to obtain confessions.

Interpol's international headquarters in Paris serves not only as centralized archives for the permanent storage of sensitive data on individuals or groups, but as a relay point allowing member countries to exchange information from each other's secret files. In the U.S. these files include the massive FBI records computerized in the National Crime Information Center (NCIC); the Treasury Enforcement Communications System (TECS); and various interfacing data banks operated by such federal agencies as the Internal Revenue Service, the Defense Department, and others.

There are at present no enforceable guidelines limiting the kind nor amount of information about U.S. citizens that can be disseminated to foreign police. The same is true of Interpol's British arm, which is fully integrated with Scotland Yard, where it is insulated against public scrutiny.

Once information, whether accurate or false, has been permanently stored in the files of Interpol's international bureau in Paris, it can be rewritten, summarized and/or passed on to any or all of the 122 member countries without permission of the originating bureau.

No matter what laws the U.S. Congress or the British Parliament may pass with respect to the confidentiality of the material, such statutes will not be binding on Interpol's General Secretariat.

During the war years, Interpol was taken over and operated by Heinrich Himmler's secret police. The impact of that Nazi period is still apparent. The radio network, the colour-tab dossier system, the practice of preventative surveillance —

these and other features persist today. As late as 1968, the Interpol General Assembly elected a former Nazi SS officer, Paul Dickopf, as president of the organization.

The KGB connection

In a bid to establish itself as an official international body, Interpol has sought to give the impression that it is part of the United Nations structure. The fact is that in 1971, the Economic and Social Council of the U.N. granted Interpol a consultative status as a *non-governmental* association.

In the opinion of some observers even that liaison raises some serious questions. The United Nations has, over the past two decades, continued to provide an important operational base for Communist espionage in the United States.

John Barron reports that a top-secret textbook used in the KGB Higher Intelligence School 101 stresses the value of the United Nations as an ideal centre for clandestine activities. The instruction manual shows the larval spies how to take advantage of the various special U.N. agencies to carry out their intelligence missions.

During former U.N. Secretary General U Thant's tenure, his personal advisor for years was Viktor M. Lassiovsky, who turned out to be a KGB officer. A number of other Soviet nationals have been expelled for spying.

In America there is a fully justified uneasiness that information on U.S. citizens may be relayed through Interpol to those Communist countries that are members. These include Rumania, Yugoslavia, Cuba, Laos, Sri Lanka, Khmer, and Vietnam.

A number of other member states have close relations with the Soviet Union and are consistently anti-Western in their international posture. They are: Ghana, Indonesia, Nigeria, Somalia, Guinea (where the Russians hope to build a secret, operational base for submarines); Tanzania, Algeria, Libya,

Kenya, and Mali.

Although Interpol points to its constitution and general regulations as a guarantee against abuses, the truth is that no machinery exists for disciplining or expelling members who violate the rules.

Interpol maintains that its services are essential for the apprehension and return of international criminals who, in these times of jet travel, have left the scene of their crime. Factually, criminal fugitives are sent back to the country where they are wanted by the police only after an extradition hearing, which formally involves both governments and courts.

That is the case where an extradition treaty actually exists between the countries concerned. But the U.S. has extradition treaties with only 27 out of 137 nations recognized as being independent states. Great Britain has concluded treaties with only 44 other countries.

Even when an extradition treaty exists, it can be applied only to those offenses which both countries recognize as a crime. This means that, as a former chief of Interpol's U.S. bureau admitted, there are few crimes for which the criminal can be extradited. They include murder, rape, narcotic trafficking, child stealing, robbery, counterfeiting and kidnapping.

Acts of terrorism and the hijacking of aircraft — the two most serious international crimes today — have only recently been added to the list, mostly by Western democracies.

As for Interpol, that organization approached the whole subject on tiptoe, declaring that such crimes are "political," and for Interpol to become involved would violate Article 3 of its constitution.

At least four Interpol member states — Algeria, Syria, Cuba, and Libya — have actually offered asylum to some of the most notorious of the terrorists and hijackers in recent years.

What, then, is the principal function of Interpol?

In brief, it is the collection, storage, and re-transmission of information and police intelligence on a universal scale.

Its massive files are not yet computerized for instantaneous retrieval of data, but they will be in the not too distant future. Interpol's Orwellian dream is to possess a third or fourth generation computer plugged into the far-flung, interfacing systems of the U.S. and other industrialized nations, as well as the European Informatics Network *(Réseau Informatique Européen)* currently in the development stage. The latter will eventually serve an operational system of high-speed communication between computers in leading European cities.

No built-in controls

The reader may well ask: is there any hope for placing effective restraints on this infant monster before it grows too big to control?

Frankly, not much. Manufacturers of computer systems have given more thought to utility than to security. The more optimistic technologists tell us that researches have produced the necessary hardware and software techniques for protecting confidential information against unauthorized access or modification. But one has to be cautious about going along with scientists — those jolly fellows. You may set out for Rainbow City and end up in Hiroshima.

In any case, as one forthright electronics expert has pointed out, a 100% secure rating will remain meaningless as long as the human element is involved. "The programmer, the operator, and the maintenance man all pose a very real threat to system security. . . . In short, you can build locks, *but who gets the keys?*"[1]

Congressional oversight? To paraphrase one of the more controversial Presidents, don't ever mention that phrase in this goddamned office again. There is no known instance in which Congressional committees have eliminated or even slowed down for a very long time the excesses of those governmental agencies over which they were supposed to exercise authority. I have absolutely no faith that they will do any better in the future.

At the same time, unless one is a complete defeatist, it is necessary to attempt some kind of solutions to the problems, even if they prove to be only stop-gap measures.

In the case of Interpol, I believe the following recommendations are minimal:

The U.S. Congress, and Parliaments in other democratic countries, should enact legislation specifically forbidding the dissemination beyond national boundaries of any non-criminal information, except the necessary data needed for identification.

Data transmitted should include only conviction records of persons found guilty by a court of competent jurisdiction, or who plead guilty to a serious crime such as those named in extradition treaties.

Unverified information such as that retained in most police dossiers — tips, allegations, rumors, and so on — should be rigorously proscribed.

Interpol's National Central Bureaux should immediately design and implement a realistic programme for purging their files at stated, brief intervals, or upon presentation of documentary evidence that they contain false or ambiguous information. This procedure should be subject to review by an independent commission, established under law.

Any individual or group not under indictment or for whom there is an outstanding warrant of arrest, should have access to their files for inspection and to petition correction if they find it inaccurate. The refusal of access on the grounds that an investigation is in progress (the pleading that has seriously undermined the Freedom of Information Acts in America) should be excluded.

Access to the contents of any NCB file (as well as the master files at the General Secretariat) should be strictly limited to authorized personnel, and punitive measures provided for those who are implicated directly or indirectly in leaking information to outside terminals.

No requests for data from any source other than a criminal justice agency should be acted upon. Even those agencies having legal access should be carefully scrutinized if they belong to countries having political police.

The various NCBs and the international bureau should maintain a record of all requests for information, including the date on which it was supplied, to whom, for what purpose, and any follow-up communication from the requesting agency.

Ultimately, the only real safeguard against the threat of a dossier-based dictatorship is the will of the people to resist every increment of power that leads in that direction.

One would like to believe that the lessons of the past few years will arouse public reaction sufficiently to stay the unlimited development of the present totalitarian potential. But I fear that no such expectation is justified. The masses have no desire for — indeed, they fear — responsibility and freedom. Today they are manipulated; tomorrow they will be programmed.

I foresee the day, before this century is out, when total surveillance, and therefore total control, of whole populations is a reality.

When that time comes, perhaps we the older ones, spending a quiet hour or two with friends in some "safe" place like our garden or the seashore, will recall the present period as the Indian Summer of our liberty.

With our voices covered by strains of some half-forgotten music, we may even try to explain to youthful robots what it was like in the good old days, when we were free to think and to speak as we wished; and dissent was a fact of daily life.

Reference Notes

Chapter 1: The Dirty Dossier

1. *FBI Law Enforcement Bulletin,* January, 1974.
2. *Computer World,* July 17, 1974.
3. *Ottowa Journal,* September 19, 1974.
4. *FBI Law Enforcement Bulletin,* op. cit.
5. *Los Angeles Times,* October 14, 1974.
6. *Interpol Annual Report,* FY '73.
7. *Time* Magazine, October 13, 1975.
8. See *Hidden Story of Scientology.* Citadel Press, 1975.

Chapter 2: EDP: "The Quiet Peril"

1. Warner, Malcolm and Stone, Michael, *The Data Bank Society.* London, 1970.
2. *New York Times,* December 27, 1970.
3. Westin, Alan F., *Privacy and Freedom.* New York, 1967.
4. Hoffman, Lance J., *Security and Privacy in Computer Systems.* Los Angeles, 1973.
5. *Encyclopedia Britannica Yearbook,* 1974.
6. Statement made to Ben A. Franklin, *New York Times,* December 27, 1970.
7. *Hearings, Senate Subcommittee on Administrative Practice and Procedure* (Invasions of Privacy), page 436.
8. *International Criminal Police Review.* November 1967.
9. *Report of a Special Subcommittee on the International Court of Justice and the International Criminal Police Organization.* Washington, 1959.

Chapter 3: The Accretion of Dangerous Power

1. Under the Napolenic type of administration in France, the police were omnipresent, their thumbs in every pot.
2. Criminologists and diplomatic representatives from the following countries attended the 1923 Vienna Congress: Austria, Belgium, Czechoslovakia, Denmark, Egypt, Fiume, France, Ger-

many, Greece, Holland, Hungary, Italy, Japan Latvia, Poland, Rumania, Sweden, Switzerland, Turkey, and the U.S.
3. Soderman, Harry, *Policeman's Lot*. London, 1959.

Chapter 4: Interpol Under Nazi Control

1. Wartime members of the Nazi-controlled Interpol were: Denmark, Bulgaria, Spain, Finland, Hungary, Italy, Rumania, Switzerland, Belgium, Czechoslovakia, Sweden, Norway, Portugal, Austria, Greece, Holland, Croatia, Turkey.
2 .*The German Police*. Supreme Hq., Allied Expeditionary Force, Evaluation and Dissemination Section. London, 1945.
3. *Newsweek,* August 7, 1944, p. 44.
4. *Encyclopedia Britannica*, 15th edition, 1974.
5. Kogon, Eugen, *The Theory and Practice* of Hell. London, 1950.
6 .Delarue, Jacques, The History of the Gestapo. London, 1964.
7. Related by Herman Rauschning in *Hitler Told Me,* and cited in Jean-Michel Angebert's *The Occult and the Third Reich*. N.Y., 1974.
8. Kogon, Eugen, *op. cit.*
9. Kogon, Eugen, *op cit.*
10. Kersten, Felix, *The Kersten Memoirs, 1940-1945*. Garden City, N.Y., 1947.
11. Hoettle, Wilhelm, *The Secret Front,* London, 1953.
12. *Ibid.*, p. 42.
13. *The Trials of the Major War Criminals.* Proceedings of the International Military Tribunal Sitting at Nuremberg, Germany. Part 12, p. 288. London, 1947.
14. Soderman, Harry, *op. cit.*
15. Hoettl, Wilhelm, *op. cit.*

Chapter 5: Twilight of the Beasts

1. *New York Times*. May 25, 1945.
2 .Hoettl, Wilhelm, *The Secret Front*. London, 1953.
3. Hoettl, Wilhelm, *op. cit.*
4. *International Criminal Police Review*. April, 1950.

Chapter 6: The International Big Brotherhood

1. *New York Times*, September 10, 1945, p. 8.

2 .The 17 countries officially represented at the reorganizational meeting were: Belgium, Chile, Denmark, Egypt, France, Great Britain, Holland, Iran, Luxembourg, Norway, Poland, Portugal, Sweden, Czechoslovakia, Turkey, and Yugoslavia.

3. Freedom, February-April, 1975. Also, *New York Times*, October 17, 1973.

Chapter 7: Keeping Tabs on the World

1. Stated in an interview with Vaughn Young, director of research for the National Commission on Law Enforcement and Social Justice.

2. Letter inserted in transcript of *Hearings, Senate Subcommittee of Committee on Appropriations*, May 6, 1975.

3. After the serious leaks in top-secret papers, President Nixon told his aide Erlichman, "Don't ever let me hear anyone say 'top-secret' in this goddamned office again."

4. *Hearings*, op. cit.

Chapter 8: The Hoover Legacy

1. *Los Angeles Times*, October 8, 1975.
2. Cited in *No Place to Hide*, by Alan Le Mond and Ron Fry. N.Y., 1975.
3. *Toronto Star*, May 5, 1973.
4. *New York Times*, June 7, 1975.
5. *New York Times*, February 25, 1974.
6. An English translation of the manual appears in John Barron's *KGB: The Secret Work of Soviet Secret Agents*. London, 1974.
7. *Time*, August 11, 1975.
8. Article by Mark Lane, in *Los Angeles Free Press*, August 9, 1968.
9. *Toronto Sun*, February 3, 1975.
10. *Newsweek*, February 9, 1975.
11. *Time*, August 27, 1973.
12. *Newsweek*, February 9, 1973.
13. *New York Times*, February 6, 1974.
14. UPI article in the *Las Vegas Sun*, July 3, 1974.
15. Memorandum from Paul H. Wright to IRS Assistant Commissioner (Compliance), dated October 23, 1969.
16. Le Mond, Alan and Fry, Ron, *No Place To Hide*. N.Y., 1975.
17. *Honolulu Star-Bulletin*, April 24, 1974.

18. Westin, Alan F. and Baker, Michael A., *Databanks In a Free Society*. Report of the National Academy of Sciences.

Chapter 9: The IRS Connection

1. At this writing, it is rumored that there are plans to move the Interpol NCB to the Department of Justice, which has legal responsibility for it, a responsibility it delegated to Treasury.
2. Diogenes, *The April Game*. Chicago, 1973.
3. Irey, Elmer, *The Tax Dodgers*. N.Y., 1949.
4. *Hearings, Senate Judiciary Subcommittee on Administrative Practice and Procedure*. 1965.
5. Diogenes, *op. cit.*
6. *Miami News*, March 14, 1975; also, *New York Times*, March 15, 1975.
7. *Los Angeles Times*, March 23, 1975.
8. Congressional Record, March 18, 1975.
9. Friedrich, Carl J., *in Totalitarianism in Perspective*. London, 1969.
10. *Los Angeles Times*, April 7, 1975.

Chapter 10: Squad 3: Interpol in Britain

1. Laurie, Peter, *Scotland Yard*. London, 1972.
2. *Essential Law For Journalists*. London, 1974.
3. *London Daily Mail*, September 11, 1975.
4. *Police Review*, May 1972.
5. Lord Stonham's statement, cited by J. Jacob in *Computer Weekly*, September 25, 1969, was: "It is an immense concept, and will entail storing far more information than any comparable project in the world."
6. Rule, James B., *Private Lives and Public Surveillance*. London, 1973.
7. *New Statesman*, May 3, 1974.
8. Rule, James B, *Op. cit.*
9. Cited in Reith, Charles, *The Blind Eye of History*. London, 1952.
10. *City News Service*, quoted in *Freedom*, March-May, 1975.
11. *Hansard*, May 21, 1975, Col. 1577.
12. Hoehne, Heinz, *Order of the Death's Head*. London, 1969.
13. *Freedom* (U.K. Edition), April-May, 1974.
14. *Hansard*, December 3, 1969.

15. *London Daily Mirror*, April 26, 1973.
16. In a letter to Arthur Lewis, M.P.

Chapter 11: The Orwellian Dream

1. International Criminal Police Review, August-September, 1975.
2. Letter from Jean Nipote, Secretary General of Interpol, to David B. Gaiman, director of the Ministry of Public Affairs, Church of Scientology.
3. *World Survey*, September 1971.
4. *I.C.P.C. Circular Letter* No. 6159/BUDIF, dated November 7, 1952.
5. Lühy, Herbert, *The State of France*. London, 1955.
6. Stead, Philip John, *The Police of Paris*. London, 1955.
7. Interview with Vaughn Young, 1976
8. Statement issued by the National Central Bureau of Interpol, Washington.
9. Interview with Vaughn Young, December 9, 1975.
10. Report of an investigator for the Church of Scientology.
11. A report by Rabbi Kaplan, cited in *The Destruction of the European Jews*. Chicago, 1961.

Chapter 12: The Devil's Rhetoric

1. Edmonton Journal, September 3, 1974. Prof. Buckner heads the sociology department of Sir George Williams University.
2. Wertham, Frederic, M.D., *A Sign For Cain*. London, 1968.
3. Wertham, Frederic, *op. cit.*, p. 180.
4. Cited in the trial of the major German war criminals. *Proceedings of the International Military Tribunal*. Part 6, page 131.